GETTING SALES

GETTING SALES
A getting-into-business guide

Dan Kennedy

Self-Counsel Press
(*a division of*)
International Self-Counsel Press Ltd.
Canada   U.S.A.

HD·
62.5
K465
1991

Printed in Canada

First edition: November, 1991

Canadian Cataloguing in Publication Data
Kennedy, Dan S., 1954-
Getting Sales
(Self-counsel business series)
0-88908-984-1
1. New business enterprises. 2. Sales promotion.
I. Title. II.Series.
HD62.5.K454 1991   658.1'1   C91-091736-1

Cover photo by Comnet/Image Finders, Vancouver.

Self-Counsel Press
(*a division of*)
International Self-Counsel Press Ltd.
Head and Editorial Office
1481 Charlotte Road
North Vancouver, British Columbia V7J 1H1

U.S. Address
1704 N. State Street
Bellingham, Washington 98225

CONTENTS

SAMPLES

TABLE

INTRODUCTION
WHY BUSINESSES FAIL

Failure. A very unpleasant thought — an even more unpleasant reality. In the typical initial period of optimism that comes with getting a new business off the ground, the idea of failure is pushed away, suppressed in the distant recesses of the mind. As a new entrepreneur, you expect success. Otherwise, why would you be doing what you're doing?

Later, when an infant business is in trouble, when warning bells should be ringing, the entrepreneur often goes into denial, sitting there, rationalizing the way things are, and insisting that they'll change for the better any day now.

A little later still, when things have gone from bad to worse to nearly irreversible, the entrepreneur still sits there, now paralyzed by fear and indecision, while the walls crumble around him or her.

Make no mistake about it, this scenario is played out more often than not. Even though the success rate of new, small businesses has actually improved a little in recent years, the disaster scenario I have just sketched is the experience of hundreds of thousands of people every year. Some just close up shop and slink away quietly in the night. Others are more severely damaged: lost savings, ruined credit, home in foreclosure, bankruptcy, and so on. Go and spend a couple days in a bankruptcy court listening to the cases called and discussed at a rapid-fire pace; it is not a pretty sight.

As a result of the kind of discussion I've just led you through, I'm sometimes introduced, as a speaker, as "the Professor of Harsh Reality." There are a lot of militant positive thinkers who insist on ignoring reality, but if you take the time to really study and analyze successful individuals and successful businesses you'll find that real, lasting success has as its foundation a firm grip on reality . So I prefer to face it and confront it. I think you need to understand how to prepare to prevent failure.

There are all sorts of theories about why businesses fail. Many people will tell you it is because of the difficulty of getting capital, yet I have seen a great many businesses grow and prosper in spite of a grievous lack of financial resources. Another popular refrain chalks up small business failure to a lack of managerial expertise, but the majority of the businesses I'm familiar with that have been built from scratch to substantial success are led by entrepreneurs with no previous managerial expertise. We even joke in my own office that I'm president of my companies because I'm woefully unqualified to be anything else. One CEO of a 500-million-dollar enterprise once told me, "It's a good thing I started this company. Today I probably couldn't get hired here!"

The truth as I know it is that the acceptance of the importance of selling, the willingness to sell, and the ability to sell more frequently makes or breaks an entrepreneur and his or her business than any other single factor. Businesses fail when businesspeople fail to sell.

This book is all about selling in its various forms — advertising, marketing, promotion, publicity, customer service. If one book in the Getting-into-Business set is more important than the others, this is the one. Sales are not going to "just happen" in sufficient quantity to support your business. You have to make sales happen.

I find it disturbing when someone thinks that he or she can operate a business reactively rather than proactively, that somehow customers will just appear and then we will take care of them. There the business owner sits, behind the counter or behind the desk, waiting for customers to call or come in. What's wrong with this picture? Everything! The greatest favor you can do for yourself as a small business owner is to make up your mind to personally and proactively makes sales happen.

In mid-1991, I attended a special business-to-business marketing conference and was shocked to learn that the majority of U.S. corporations have customer service under control of their administrative and operations people, not under the control of their marketing people! They do not understand the link between getting sales and customer service. They view it as an expense, not an investment. They account for it in their operations budgets rather than their marketing budgets. They are wrong.

This book is totally devoted to learning how to effectively choose, mix, and use every method and opportunity for getting sales that is appropriate for your particular business, product, or service. Some of the most important of these are the following:

(a) Marketing. In its largest, broadest sense, getting sales is done through marketing, which I often define as the delivery of the right message to the right market via the right media. Your message is a mix of the products and services you sell, the benefits those products and services offer to the customer, your own credibility and image, your pricing, your guarantees, and your customer service policies. Your message summarizes all those things and more. And your message may and probably will change from time to time and from market segment to market segment. For example, if you were marketing a fast-food restaurant, you might craft one message for those times when you were trying to reach children and a different message for when you were trying to reach their parents.

(b) Advertising and publicity. Getting sales involves advertising, the use of media to get your message to different prospects. Publicity is free advertising that uses the same media that paid advertising does.

(c) Distribution. Getting sales is also done through distribution. You'll be choosing among options such as retailing, wholesaling, sales agents, mail-order, and other means of getting products together with consumers. One of my goals in this book is to expand your thinking about the different ways you can distribute your products.

(d) Customer service. Customer service is a major and often overlooked way of getting sales. Far too many businesses operate like a fire crew trying to move water down the line in a bucket with a big hole in the bottom. The bucket gets filled up at the pump, but, by the time it gets to the person ready to throw it on the fire, all the water has gone out the bottom of the bucket. A business not strongly oriented toward customer retention and satisfaction plays the same game: the bucket is filled up with new customers, through a lot of work at the pump, but by the time the bucket gets to the point of making a contribution to stability, profit, and financial security, all the customers have dropped out the bottom of the bucket!

1

ESTABLISHING AN IDENTITY

Marketing is a brick-by-brick process. Creating an identity for your business is one of the first bricks. Winning in a competitive marketplace starts with a winning identity!

As an individual, you have an identity. It incorporates your family background, education, experiences, personality, values, beliefs, personal appearance, the home and neighborhood you've chosen to live in, the car you drive, the books you read, and many other factors. The sum total is as unique and uniquely yours as your fingerprint. Identity descriptions of people are sometimes very short and simplified: he's a jock; she's a liberal. Of course, any such description, while handy, is probably unfairly simplistic. Still, we insist on creating such identity descriptions for the people in our world as a matter of convenience and as a means of communication.

Similarly, we attach identity tags to businesses or, often, we accept the tags the businesses develop and attach to themselves. For example, K-Mart has long been known as a discount store while Sears and J.C. Penney are known as family department stores, and Saks Fifth Ave. and Nieman-Marcus are known as elite department stores. Most of the merchandise will be different in these three types of stores, but you might find the same item sold in all of them, too. Today, K-Mart would like to be viewed as a peer of Sears and J.C. Penney rather than as the purveyor of cheap "blue light specials," but its identity is so fixed in the public consciousness that it will be very difficult to change.

It's smart to give a great deal of thought to the development of your business's identity, which can include the name, the logo, the slogans, the colors, the merchandise or service mix, the physical look of the store or office, and many other related factors. Combined, they'll give the public a mental imprint — they'll make up a tag. And once that tag is attached, it's tough to remove it.

a. WHAT'S IN A NAME?

Many businesspeople commit their first major identity error in naming their businesses. Although there are exceptions, in 90 percent of cases, a successful business has a name that, in some way, clearly communicates what it is and/or does.

Names that are confusing or that can be used interchangeably for different types of businesses — Jane Smith Enterprises, for example — should be avoided.

Consider these business names and how effectively they represent their businesses:

(a) Mail Boxes Etc. versus Business Service Centers

(b) Physician's Weight Loss Centers versus Health Systems Inc.

(c) CareerTrak Seminars versus Fred Cryden Associations

(d) PayLess Shoe Source versus Crown Shoes

Think about these names: Dunkin' Donuts, Midas Muffler, Classic Car Wash, Dominos Pizza Delivers. I believe that the best possible business name telegraphs what the business is, does, or offers.

b. LOGOS

Many new businesspeople just can't seem to wait. They run to an ad agency or graphic artist and invest several hundred to several thousand dollars in a logo design. Most businesses *can* benefit from a logo — a symbol that becomes known and recognized by the public. But it's not a necessity. I favor logos that are simple in design and directly related to the theme of the business. Also, keep in mind that you'll want to use your logo in a variety of places, sizes, and, probably, colors: how will the logo you're considering look if shrunk by 200 percent to fit in the corner of your business card? Or enlarged by 2,000 percent to go on a billboard?

I like to see people keep logo design costs to a minimum. There are a number of software programs in the desktop publishing/graphics area that let you develop logos right on your own computer.

If you must get professional help, look for a freelance commercial or graphic artist and stay away from advertising agencies. Don't be afraid to shop around and to frankly discuss price. Also, insist that your deal with the artist include all the revisions needed to satisfy you for one agreed-upon price.

Another option to consider, depending on your business, is the use of your own photograph as your identifying image instead of a logo. Salespeople in many fields, models, chiropractors, dentists, and other professionals go this route, and it's applicable to a broad spectrum of small business.

c. WHAT ABOUT COLORS?

If you intend to incorporate certain theme colors into your business identity, there are a number of things to consider. How will the colors work in the store or office environment? In print? Are they different from the colors of major competitors? Are they so unique that printers and other vendors will charge extra to supply them? Also, what are the psychological ramifications of the colors? How appropriate are they to your business? Bright red or orange might be more appropriate for a discount hardware store than an upscale beauty salon for example.

You'll notice that many national franchisers stick to very simple color themes. Midas Muffler uses gold and black; Burger King, red and yellow; Kentucky Fried Chicken, red and white. Sticking to such basic colors helps keep costs down.

While I think there's a danger in getting too carried away with this, there has been a considerable amount of research done on the impact of different colors and color combinations on consumers when used in advertising, store interiors, office interiors, and product package designs. For example, in direct-mail packages with multiple enclosures, you'll often find the order form printed on yellow or pink; both have been found to be "high response" colors. In one instance where I tested a white order form, yellow order form, and pink order form against one another, all other factors being equal, pink out-pulled white by about 100 percent and out-pulled yellow by about 20 percent. That's an example of something you could learn only through experimentation or, possibly, ferreting out and reading the research that's been done on this subject. Fortunately, most of this is not quite as mysterious and can be figured out with plain, simple common sense.

Red, for example, is an action color. It draws the eye better than any other color, but it also tends to make the mind race a little bit. A lot of red can be disturbing or even alarming, probably thanks to the association with fire, fire engines, and stop signs. You might want to use red as a theme color for a fast food business or a retail store like a hardware store or an auto parts store. You probably would not want to incorporate red as a theme color for a classy jewelry store or beauty salon. Conversely, blue is a cool color, associated with sky, water, and ice, and can be effectively used for up-scale retail operations, like jewelry stores, or professional offices, like stockbrokers'.

I do not believe in hard rules for this, but you may find the following chart in Sample #1 useful as a thought-starter in deciding which colors to use.

d. POSITIONING

The word "positioning" is advertising jargon, but the concept is important. Avis is number two. They try harder. This is Avis's position; they have cleverly taken a disadvantage, the fact that another company is bigger and better known, and turned it to an advantage by pointing out that number twos try harder and will, by implication, serve you better than the "big guy." Dominos took the position of "the" deliverer of pizza in 30 minutes or less. Pizza Hut is giving them a run for their money, but, still, if you ask any ten people to respond to "pizza delivery," eight will pop out with "Dominos."

As you put together your business's identity and marketing message, you are positioning your business in the market. One of the definitions of positioning is how your customers and prospective customers think and feel about your business in comparison to other similar businesses competing for their attention. So, as you decide on your positioning, consider how you want your market to view you.

A brilliant positioning job has been done by the small but very successful chain of stores called Our Secret — Jewelers To The Stars. This chain sells classy costume jewelry — gold-plated, not solid gold; cubic zirconiums, not diamonds — not unlike the costume jewelry you can buy in any jewelry store and most department stores. But Our Secret has taken a distinctively different position, presenting their products as replicas and can't-tell-the-difference duplicates of solid gold and diamond jewelry, not as costume jewelry. They have furnished jewelry to movie and TV shows, including "Dynasty," and they use this fact to establish themselves as the jewelers to the stars. As a result, they attract a different clientele and generally command higher prices.

SAMPLE #1
COLOR USAGE CHART

Color	Associations	Frequent Uses/Users
Red	Fire, heat; action, excitement. "Sale." Important. Danger.	Fast food. Auto hardware. Advertising of sales.
Blue	Cool, cold. Sophisticated, classy. Businesslike, professional.	Financial services, professional practice.
"Soft" tones: blues, maroon, gray, mauve, off-white.	Relaxing, calming, secure, reassuring. Quiet.	Beauty parlors and salons. jewelry and fashion stores. health care clinics.
Green	Nature, outdoors. Money. Military.	Florists, lawn and garden stores, golf courses, resorts. Moneymaking offers, real estate investment.
Yellow	Caution. Sunshine, sunny, bright. Health.	Travel, summer/outdoor activities. Health foods, health products. Service businesses.
"Earth" tones: brown, rust, orange, yellow, tan, beige.	Calm. Sedate. Maturity Nature, natural.	Libraries, dens. Older age groups. Restaurants and lounges, clothing stores, legal and accounting offices.
"Miami Vice" colors: pink, green, turquoise, brilliant white, bright blue.	Hip, exciting, new. Young.	Restaurants, clothing stores, beauty salons.
"Hi-tech" colors: silver, dark blue, steel-gray, metallics	Technology, science. Future	Computer-related businesses, electronics stores and dealers, night clubs.

One of their competitors, Imposters, is successfully telling the same basic story but emphasizing their duplicates of specific pieces of expensive jewelry.

I urge you to think very carefully about the position that you carve out for yourself in the market. With creative positioning, you can give an ordinary business an extraordinary marketing advantage!

To make your positioning effective, follow these three rules:

(a) Keep it focused: concentrate on what your company does well.

(b) Keep it consistent: apply your positioning consistently to every aspect of your business.

(c) Keep it long term: avoid changing your positioning during the early phases. Give your customer time to become aware of your company, try your product or service, and reward you with repeat business.

e. YOUR BEST POTENTIAL CUSTOMER

When determining your desired position or establishing an identity in the marketplace, you need to know who you are marketing to. Who do you imagine as your best potential customers? To learn about your best potential customers, you need to understand their demographics, lifestyle, and media use.

1. Demographics

Demographics will tell you very specific information about the market you want to capture. For example, demographics can give you information about potential customers' —

(a) age,

(b) marital status,

(c) sex,

(d) income,

(e) race,

(f) home ownership versus renting,

(g) household size,

(h) number of children, etc.

This is just the type of information collected by the U.S. Census Bureau and Statistics Canada, so you can use their statistics for your demographics research.

2. Lifestyle

Demographics won't tell you anything about your customer's lifestyle or what he or she thinks. For example, what are your customer's attitudes and political beliefs? How does this person spend money? Once you have a picture of that person's lifestyle, or "psychographics," you'll know what their values are, too.

3. Media use

If you want your customer to know about your product, you've got to know how to reach him or her. What media does he or she use? If you want to advertise on TV to reach working women, you won't advertise during the daytime soaps. Are your customers night-shift workers? Late night radio might be the best way of reaching them. Find out which media your customers prefer and then plan your advertising campaign accordingly.

For a more extensive discussion on positioning and determining your market, see *The Advertising Handbook,* another title in the Self-Counsel Series.

2

THE SEVEN-STEP ADVERTISING PLAN

Chances are, you are not an advertising expert and do not have the time or inclination to become one. The trick for most entrepreneurs is to simplify this inherently complex part of business as much as possible. The seven-step plan described here is not the only or most comprehensive approach to advertising. It is intentionally stripped down, streamlined, and simplified for your benefit. It is enough to lay the next few bricks.

I am unceasingly amazed at the businesspeople who take a cavalier attitude toward advertising even though they spend a fortune on it. I've watched small-business owners carelessly and hurriedly throw together a Yellow Pages ad that's going to cost them $1,000 a month!

One of the most profitable things you can possibly do as an entrepreneur is to become an avid, dedicated, curious student of advertising. In the appendix, you'll find a long list of books and other materials you can use to learn about advertising, and I urge you to devour every single one of them. For many businesses, advertising will be or should be one of your top five expense categories, and yet it's too often the one that business owners know the least about.

The great success educator Earl Nightingale once observed, in one of his daily radio broadcasts, that anyone could become an internationally recognized expert in just about any chosen field with about an hour a day of dedicated study for two to three years. It would be a very good idea to invest your hour a day in learning about advertising.

To get going immediately, here are the seven parts of a sound, sensible approach to small-business advertising:

(a) Establish specific goals and objectives

(b) Determine what you will advertise

(c) Determine what you can invest into advertising

(d) Choose the appropriate medium

(e) Prepare your advertising message

(f) Place your advertising in the chosen medium

(g) Evaluate the effectiveness of your advertising

a. ESTABLISH SPECIFIC GOALS AND OBJECTIVES

What do you want to achieve with your advertising? Incidentally, for many businesses, success with advertising will be break-even. If advertising can provide a new customer at break-even, and you can then profit from that customer's repeat business and referrals, you have the foundation for a continually growing, profitable business.

b. DETERMINE WHAT YOU WILL ADVERTISE

Is there a particular product or service that stands out above the others you offer, that is of greater appeal to a greater number of people? Will you use a loss-leader? Should you emphasize price, service, quality, or product uniqueness?

c. DETERMINE WHAT YOU CAN INVEST INTO ADVERTISING

How much can you and will you invest in your advertising campaign? You may decide on either a percentage of your income or a particular set amount.

Think in terms of 3- to 12-month spans and commitments. Many businesspeople err in advertising sporadically and only when they desperately need a surge of sales. But advertising works best when it's a consistent part of your business. You also need to remember that there are two pay-offs from advertising: direct pay-off, from a new customer who calls or comes in the door and says "I'm here because of the ad I saw in Tuesday's paper," and indirect pay-off, from a customer who comes in after exposure to a lot of your advertising, over a period of time. The indirect pay-off or what we might call the cumulative influence of advertising comes about only through consistent use of advertising.

d. CHOOSE THE APPROPRIATE MEDIUM

Here, some testing will probably be required to determine what works best for your particular business. However, common sense will go a long way in sorting out media. Radio spots, for example, will logically be more appropriate for advertising an upcoming weekend sale at a car dealership than for advertising sophisticated financial planning services for high-income professionals.

A simple idea I often suggest to business owners struggling to choose the right advertising media is to phone owners of similar businesses in faraway geographic areas (so that they are not competitors) and ask them about what they're using that works. When you attend conventions and conferences, such as trade association meetings, you can ask these questions, too.

Incidentally, some media are much better suited to direct, immediate response than others. Many businesspeople do not understand this, so you need to take others' advice — and even their reports of what works and what doesn't — with the proverbial grain of salt. And you need to choose media that match your objectives.

For example, flying the Goodyear blimp over a stadium is institutional or image advertising. People don't leave the stadium at halftime to run down to the Goodyear store and buy tires because they just saw the blimp. If Goodyear wanted to create a surge of tire sales in their stores, they would use a sale ad in the newspaper, a coupon promotion, or direct mail to past customers. Institutional/image advertising has its place in every business's mix, but you need to understand which media work best for it versus which can generate immediate response, and then use them appropriately.

In the early months of most businesses, almost all the available ad dollars should be invested in direct-response media and campaigns, so as to recover and turn over those dollars rapidly and frequently. A $500 budget turned over three times in the same month is really a $1,500 ad budget for the month.

As a business matures and hits certain cash flow and income benchmarks, you can begin gradually and modestly decreasing the commitments to direct response and diverting funds to institutional advertising. Institutional advertising is a way of long-term investing.

Here is a list of commonly used media, with some comments about each option.

1. Yellow Pages

For most businesses, advertising in the main Yellow Pages serving their market area is not just an option but a virtual necessity. And Yellow Pages advertising quite often delivers the best return on investment.

Companies that market nationally, not just locally, can use Yellow Pages in major markets all across the country. You do not have to have a store or office in a particular city in order to advertise in that city's Yellow Pages.

I believe that every business needs a presence in the local Yellow Pages, and that many businesses ought to consider advertising in the Yellow Pages of other key cities, as well.

2. Newspapers

Advertising in most daily or Sunday metropolitan newspapers is too expensive for many businesses. A small local business may find value in a strategy of frequent small ads. One technique is to use a small ad in the newspaper to refer to your larger, more complete ad in the Yellow Pages.

Many communities also have small, weekly newspapers that concentrate on reporting community news and events. These newspapers have a surprisingly large readership and often represent bargain advertising opportunities. They will also usually let you run "advertorials," advertisements made to look and read like articles about your business, or they'll give you editorial coverage when you buy space advertising. These "articles" are usually read more than conventional ads.

3. Coupon-pack direct mail

Coupon packs or co-op mailings with a number of different merchants' coupons in them are very good for many different types of businesses. If you are using this medium for professional services or potentially high-priced sales businesses, such as dentistry, chiropractic, optometry, car dealership, furniture store, or swimming pool company, for example, you should be able to recoup your investment from the value of just one or two new customers/buyers/patients. If using it for more routine types of consumer purchases, such as fast food, car washes, fast oil change, etc., you should be able to recoup your investment from a response percentage of 1 percent to 2½ percent. If greater response is needed to recoup, then the particular coupon media you are considering is probably overpriced.

4. Radio

Radio is a very difficult direct-response media; if your ads require people to make note of an address, phone number, etc., it will take a very heavy saturation campaign to get results, and the expense may not be worth it. A lot of radio listeners are driving in their cars while listening and cannot jot down information. Radio is best for businesses with known names and lots of locations, like a chain of fast-food restaurants or supermarkets. However, radio advertising can be an effective way to call public attention to a more detailed, descriptive newspaper or Yellow Pages ad.

Radio works very well for businesses that get the radio station personalities involved as customers and spokespersons. Several entities in the weight loss industry use this strategy brilliantly.

5. Television

Television 30- and 60-second spots are useful in creating identity awareness and reinforcing other advertising, much like radio, but not particularly effective in driving direct response. For many businesses, 2-minute spots are more effective. And a growing phenomenon is the use of the 30-minute "infomercial," locally produced and aired for a local business or professional.

Television is a good choice if you have a very dramatic demonstratable product or service or if you have a TV personality as your business's spokesperson.

6. Billboards

Billboard advertising is very good for businesses with multiple locations throughout a city and/or businesses that can communicate a good marketing message with a picture and no more than ten words that people can comprehend at a glance.

7. Signage

Many businesspeople don't even think of this as an advertising medium. I am often amazed at the neglect of low-cost or free opportunities to advertise using signs on a business's own building, windows, delivery vehicles, or company cars.

8. Direct mail

Doing your own solo direct mail can be hugely effective and enormously profitable, although it may be the most difficult advertising medium to learn to use well. Self-Counsel Press publishes *A Small Business Guide to Direct Mail*, a comprehensive look at using direct mail in your business, and I teach a seminar on this topic. See the appendix for more information.

9. Other advertising media

I believe that at least 70 percent — and, in most cases, 80 percent to 90 percent — of a small business's total ad budget should go to some or all of the above eight media. The remaining small percentage can be used for a variety of less important media, such as the following:

(a) Special advertising supplements and flyers

(b) School book covers

(c) Placemats

(d) Maps with advertising

(e) High school sports programs, home show programs, etc.

(f) Bookmatches

(g) Calendars

Many local businesses — especially those that are discount or sale/event-oriented — often do well in "shoppers" or "flyers" like *Pennysaver* or *Thrifty Nickel*. Some businesses maintain regular ad schedules. Others occasionally splurge with a full-page or cover position. Some cities also have alternative weekly papers that emphasize coverage of local theater, restaurants, nightclubs, and other entertainment, and advertising in these can be very effective. In Phoenix, for example, there is a weekly called *New Times* that is probably *the* most productive media for restaurants, night clubs, specialty retailers, and many other types of businesses.

e. PREPARE YOUR ADVERTISING MESSAGE

Advertising needs, at its heart, news. Simply, you need to have something to say! Something that's newsworthy, interesting, attention-grabbing, provocative, and appealing. You don't advertise just to advertise; you advertise to get the word out about something that will excite people.

During the time I was completing this book, a sandwich bag company was massively advertising its new closure device: a strip that changes color as it seals, so you know it is sealed. As inventions go, this is not exactly of life-changing importance, but it is news, and it is important to the millions of parents who prepare kids' lunches while still bleary-eyed in the morning and package up leftovers after dinner. If you look around you and stay alert for this, you'll see the news angle in most advertising.

Of course, there's more than news to a marketing message. So how do you get your marketing message together? For many business owners, my friend and colleague Gary Halbert's advice about preparing an advertising message is a good way to start. Tape-record yourself telling people about your business, products, and services, in person or over the phone, have the tape transcribed, and then convert that content to an advertising message. Gary bases this advice on the idea that you know how to sell yourself and your products or services, you know more about it than any ad writer you might hire, and you bring a unique enthusiasm to the process that should be preserved in advertising. You may not see yourself as an ad writer, but you can pitch your own business successfully. With this process, you develop advertising that is, as Gary describes it, "salesmanship in print."

As a consultant and copywriter, I often employ this technique in developing marketing campaigns for clients. I first get them to put their best pitch on tape, I have it transcribed, and I use that as the raw material to build with. Why? Because they know more about how to sell what they sell than I could hope to learn in a reasonable length of time.

An excellent place to collect good ideas for free is the main public library in your area. There you can access Yellow Pages telephone directories, daily newspapers, and local magazines from hundreds of different cities all across the country. Also at the library are years of back issues of trade, industry, specialty, and consumer magazines. You can check out a large variety of ads for your type of business, products, or service in just a few hours.

Personally, I like to put each individual idea, phrase, slogan, offer, promise, etc., on its own 3" x 5" card. Then I sort those cards, ordering them and re-ordering them until I feel I have them in the best possible sequence. From there, I can write out a clear marketing message and compose ads, brochures, sales letters, telemarketing scripts, and so on.

There are, of course, many subtle techniques for turning that raw material into a truly great advertising message, and for that you need, as I've already advised, to really become a student of advertising.

f. PLACE YOUR ADVERTISING IN THE CHOSEN MEDIUM

The best tip I can offer here is don't pay "rate card." The rates for just about every advertising media you'll ever deal with are negotiable. You can often get first-time advertiser, test, multiple-use, and cash-payment discounts of 5 percent to 25 percent and/or concessions and freebies, like a color ink imprint free, a bigger size for the small size price, and so on.

Hinting strongly about your budget limitations will almost certainly lead to discounts and savings when buying ad space.

g. EVALUATE THE EFFECTIVENESS OF YOUR ADVERTISING

To make ever-better decisions in your advertising campaigns, you need to look closely at the results of your advertising. Most businesspeople do a miserable job of tracking the results from different ad media and campaigns and offer up a plethora of excuses — we're too busy, customers can't remember what ad they saw, etc. You cannot afford to accept these excuses. You must accurately and precisely track the results of your advertising.

I have a big warning for you here: count responses, not just orders or customers. Often, for example, a business owner will tell me that a particular ad doesn't work. But when we run it again and I closely monitor its performance, we discover that it produces a number of phone calls — but the people handling the phones "drop the ball" in getting those callers into the place of business. Advertising does have limitations; it cannot deliver new customers; it can only deliver *prospective* customers.

3

THREE GREAT WAYS TO REACH YOUR CUSTOMERS

a. DIRECT MAIL

The best thing about direct mail is that, for the moments your direct-mail letter or mailing piece is in the hands of your customer or prospect, you have no competition. With most other ad media — TV, radio, coupon packages, the Yellow Pages — the customer or prospect is bombarded by a number of pitches, one right after the other.

Admittedly, direct mail is not easy to make work. But once you have a direct-mail system that works, that brings in new customers and new sales at break-even or better, you have an immensely valuable asset. You can invest money in the system with predictable results. You can control the flow of business by the number of pieces you put in the mail. You can prevent seasonal slumps by increasing your mailings. You gain tremendous control over your acquisition of customers.

1. Start with current customers

For novices, it's usually best to start learning how to use direct mail with your present, satisfied customers rather than with new prospects. You can use direct mail to current customers to advertise special sales, offer new products and services, and stimulate repeat business or referrals. As you see what works and what doesn't with these uses of direct mail, you'll gain know-how and confidence that will be helpful to you in switching to using direct mail to generate new customers.

2. Repetition pays off

One-shot direct mail rarely pays off. It takes repetition to persuade, so the most powerful direct-mail strategy is to target a group of prospective customers and then communicate with them via a sequence of mailings.

I get quite a bit of direct mail from retailers, restaurants, and service businesses, most of which I ignore — just like most other people. But I did go and buy my eyeglasses from a new eyeglass retailer who got me via direct mail, specifically via a sequence of mailings. I got at least six different letters and flyers from this store over a few months and finally said to myself, Maybe I should try these folks.

If I were running a direct-mail campaign for a local, small business and could only budget for 10,000 pieces every quarter, I would not mail 10,000 homes once. I would find a way to choose 2,000 homes and mail to them 5 times during the calendar quarter.

3. The two-step method

You can also employ a two-step method for getting interested, qualified prospective customers to raise their hands and identify themselves, so you can direct a very thorough marketing effort to them.

You might start with the cheapest direct-mail vehicle on earth, the lowly postcard. Let's say, for the sake of example, you run a kitchen and closet remodeling company and have a very good marketing story to tell, great client references, and before/after examples. This all adds up to a lot of very persuasive information to deliver to a qualified prospect, but you don't want to waste a lot of money delivering all that information to people with no interest in remodeling their homes. To 10,000 homes, you send a simple postcard that says something like this:

If you've even been thinking about remodeling your kitchen...if the idea of new organizing systems for your closets is at all appealing to you...before you start shopping...before choosing a remodeler...before spending a dime, let us give you a free information kit, including the booklet *How to Remodel for Less!*

Just call 555-1011 and we'll send you your kit. No cost. No obligation. No salesperson will ever call.

From 10,000 randomly selected addresses, you might get only 25 responses to the postcard — but think about the value of those 25 people! They've raised their hands and said, Hey, we *are* thinking about getting some remodeling done. Now you can afford to make a significant investment in marketing to these 25 people: the kit, follow-up mailings, and maybe even a free videotape. This two-step method is a very effective, efficient, and economical way to use direct mail.

For more information on using direct mail in your business, see *A Small Business Guide to Direct Mail*, another title in the Self-Counsel Series. I have written a guide to writing effective direct-mail letters, *The Ultimate Sales Letter*. See the appendix for more information.

b. MAKING YELLOW PAGES ADVERTISING PAY OFF

For some businesses, the Yellow Pages are just about the only ad medium used. For many businesses, the Yellow Pages are the best, most productive means of advertising. For others, the Yellow Pages do not pay off, and they advertise "defensively" — because their competitors advertise there, they advertise there.

I believe that any business serving consumers and most businesses serving other businesses can make Yellow Pages advertising hugely profitable, but, to do so, they have to take a "contrarian" approach.

My approach to this type of advertising is to avoid the typical Yellow Pages ad and, instead, insert what is really a direct-response advertisement. The typical Yellow Pages ad is just a giant business card, a reference list of basic information: name, location, hours, products or services list, phone, etc. If you look through your Yellow Pages, you'll see that 99 percent of the ads fit this description and that they look very much alike. Against this norm, you'll occasionally see a very different Yellow Pages ad that could also run in a newspaper or a magazine because it is a true direct-response ad: it has a headline that telegraphs the promise of a positive benefit, a step-by-step sales story, and a clear call to action. See Sample #2 for examples.

Will anybody read all that copy? Your Yellow Pages rep will argue that there's way too much copy, that the type is too small, that there's not enough "yellow space." Your rep will be wrong.

When you are dealing with readers who are contemplating a significant investment, you can safely assume that they will welcome as much information as they can get, even if they have to squint to get it. The "Tree Doctor" ad brought a whopping 825 percent increase in calls the very first month it ran.

The chiropractor's ad, which I developed, was one of the most successful chiropractic ads in the Phoenix market in the year that it ran. It has some similarity to "normal" Yellow Pages ads but provides a lot more information than most, a headline, a complete sales story, and even testimonials.

If you compare these ads to the Yellow Pages ads in the same business categories in your own local Yellow Pages directory, the differences between these and most of the other ads will stand out.

The fourth ad, which uses all text, goes 100 percent against the norm in Yellow Pages advertising, and its approach has been copied and used effectively by many different types of

4 Reasons why you'll be thrilled with a QUALITY SpaceSpan* Patio Awning

1. You save money ... and yet get superb, long-lasting quality

It's only sensible that the first thing that comes to mind when you're planning a Patio Awning is AFFORDABILITY ... but it should NOT be at the expense of quality. And it doesn't have to be! Here's why a Patio Awning from The Extension Factory saves you money ... without sacrificing quality or workmanship! You see, being part of the massive SpaceSpan* Network, that means you enjoy our buying power and our unique construction systems. And it means you save money, AND you get your patio FASTER.

2. You get EXACTLY what you want in design and colour

You'd think having a "custom made" patio would be expensive and cause delays. NOT when you call on The Extension Factory! Here's what we'll do for you! Firstly, we'll send a professional design consultant to your home - obligation FREE - to discuss your requirements, talk colours and designs to blend with your environment, and even develop a colour sketch plan for you. At this point, YOU haven't spent a cent ... If you say, "Go Ahead" then we'll make it all happen ...

3. The professionalism and speed of our installation team

Imagine, the patio you've always dreamed of installed by friendly, experienced professionals in just a few days. Well, that's our promise to you. As an added bonus, we'll even prepare plans for Council, obtain necessary approvals and handle any other queries.

4. Space-Age Materials

The final touch to good workmanship is of course, the colour and quality of the material used in construction. Just look at the exclusive, architecturally styled materials you'll get to choose from. Manufactured to the highest possible standards, SpaceSpan* Patio Awnings are available in Colorbond Zincalume^R Steel or Aluminium. We know you'll be impressed by the quality. We guarantee you'll be impressed with the price.

ALSO
- Screened Enclosures
- Glass Enclosures
- Pool and Spa Enclosures
- Carports
- *SpaceSpan* Skylite Panels*

Specially blended acrylic panels allowing soft filtered sunlight into your patio area without glare or harmful U. V. rays.

Visit our Showroom for friendly, expert advice or phone now.
We'll be delighted to hear from you.

QUALITY YOU CAN TRUST

10 YEAR GUARANTEE

EMAIL

TEF THE EXTENSION FACTORY

24 1466

Lic. No. 51779

320 MANNS RD, WEST GOSFORD

SPACESPAN' REG TRADE MARK OF VALECTRO INDUSTRIES
A DIVISION OF THE EMAIL GROUP OF COMPANIES

Ad used with permission of Dr. Patricia Lehew, Dynamic Chiropractic, Phoenix, Arizona, and Dan S. Kennedy.

5 REASONS WHY YOU SHOULD CHOOSE THE TREE DOCTOR

1. We are fully insured ... for your peace of mind. Full workers compensation and $5 million Public Liability Insurance.

2. Qualified tradesmen ... not just "loppers". Tree care and removal is a highly technical trade. Your property and trees deserve fully trained staff.

3. We do all the work ourselves and have all our own equipment. You won't need to wait on someone else to complete the job.

4. For your guarantee of professionalism we are members of the National Arborists Association of Australia and life members of the International Society of Arboriculture.

5. We care — about your trees and about your property. *OUR SERVICES INCLUDE* consultations * removal of hazardous or unwanted trees * hazard assessment * removal of deadwood * thinning * legal reports and representation * fertilisation * injections * stump grinding * pre- and post-construction reports * transplanting * soil analysis and manipulation * staff training and education.

VALUABLE FREE BOOKLET ... with every quote or consultation.

WE SERVICE YOUR AREA ... we have clients from Wyong to Wollongong, from Bondi to Katoomba. Wherever you are it will be a pleasure to serve you. Please call us now ...

625 8000

THE TREE DOCTOR

103 Beames Ave. Rooty Hill 2766
Mobile 018 220 928 Fax 625 4220

TREES BROUGHT BACK TO GOOD HEALTH OR CAREFULLY LAID TO REST

Ad used with permission of Gary Halbert, Everett & Lloyd Advertising, Key West, Florida.

businesses over the years. As you can see, it doesn't look like an ad at all. In fact, many people mistake it for some kind of public service announcement placed by the Yellow Pages and do not realize they are reading an ad until they are into it. It pre-empts the other advertising thanks to its very different appearance.

The point of these examples is that you do not have to be bound by the constraints of the norm in Yellow Pages advertising and will often be best served by ignoring most of those rules.

Let me summarize the most important points you need to keep in mind about Yellow Pages advertising:

(a) If you have a really good ad, a larger size will usually pay off more than proportionately. For example, when you double the size of a good ad, you don't just double the response, you triple or even quadruple it. But bigger is not better in every case. Making an ineffective ad bigger will not make it work better.

(b) Your small ad can out-perform bigger ads if you follow the tips and ideas given here and the bigger advertisers don't.

(c) Given the choice between emphasizing lowest prices or best service, a compelling discussion of superior service wins every time. A price advantage only gives the prospective customer one good reason to choose you. A good description of superior service can give a number of reasons.

(d) Professionally taken, quality photographs out-pull line drawings, illustrations, or cartoons in almost every situation.

(e) Big, heavy, black reverses should be used sparingly, if at all.

(f) Red or other extra colors are of questionable value.

(g) The headline is the most important component of the ad. Use it to telegraph the promise of a benefit or benefits and/or to arouse curiosity with a startling statement or question. The examples I've given all have good headlines.

(h) Yellow Pages ads with specific offers and especially with free offers out-pull ads without offers. An ad for a plumber featuring a "free plumbing problem prevention check-up" or "checklist" or "booklet" will out-pull plumbing ads without such features.

(i) Don't feel obligated to accept advice from the Yellow Pages rep. Consider what he or she has to say, but do not be intimidated by it.

c. DIAL FOR DOLLARS

Do you know any business or home without a telephone? That's right, everybody's got one. And do you know anybody who hears the telephone ring and ignores it? Right — just about everybody responds to the phone.

I can take any business of any kind, put its owner on the phone, and generate business at essentially no cost other than time. And there's no magic to it. It's just common sense.

Let's say you've got a restaurant in need of customers. Chances are, you have a down time between the lunch rush-hour and either happy hour or dinner time. Here's what you do:

(a) Look in local directories for customers in your area. With a "criss-cross directory" (a directory by street address), available at the library, compile a list of names and phone numbers of people who live within easy driving distance of your restaurant.

(b) During your daily down time, phone those people. Many won't be at home and some will rudely hang up on you, but some will be home and will listen to you courteously.

(c) Deliver a little verbal ad that you've written. It might go something like this:

> Hi, I'm Arnie Bezikarus, owner of the Bezikarus Greek Restaurant near your home, at 7th Street and Waters Boulevard. I'd like to offer you a free dinner. Do you have just a few minutes for my call?

The person says yes, and you continue:

> I'm calling some of our nearby neighbors, to extend my personal invitation to come in and find out how enjoyable a homemade, authentic Greek feast can be. Do you like Greek food?

If the person says no, you give a brief commentary on what Greek food is like, how good it is, etc., and then make your offer. If the person says yes, you make the offer:

> Any evening, Monday through Thursday, this week or next, I'll give you one dinner free with the purchase of any dinner at a regular price. To take advantage of this offer, you can make a reservation now or call back in later. Your name is on our invited guest list and we'll be looking for your call. Do you think you'll be joining us one of these evenings?

As you can see, this kind of advertising campaign is not difficult, not high pressure or offensive, and not particularly time-consuming — the average completed call takes only a few minutes — but consider the impact on the neighborhood restaurant that serves, say, 30 dinners per weeknight. Telemarketing industry statistics indicate that you can average about 30 dialings and 5 to 10 completed calls to residences per hour, so in a day's down-time hours, you might actually talk with 10 or 15 people; in a week, 50 to 75 people. You should be able to get about 20 percent of these people to come in — 10 out of 50, 15 out of 75. In a month, you could expose 40 to 60 new customers to your restaurant, in a year 400 to 600. Assuming you're doing a good job at the restaurant, many of these people should become repeat customers. If just 100 come back at least 3 times, that's the equivalent of 10 weeknights filled. If 300 come back at least 3 times, that's the equivalent of 1 whole month filled. Could these numbers make the difference between a neighborhood restaurant failing or succeeding? Absolutely!

Obviously, any business can apply this idea. You could also hire people to do telemarketing for you, working at your place of business or from their homes. Your business might even be able to use of a telemarketing machine. An auto-dialing machine can call hundreds of numbers, delivering a recorded message to those who answer and stay on the line.

4

OTHER MARKETING TECHNIQUES

There are many ways a business owner can improve sales other than by heavy advertising or expensive campaigns. This chapter outlines a few of these ideas for marketing your business without spending a lot of dollars.

a. NETWORK

I know three businesspeople who belong to the same chamber of commerce. Two complain that they never get any business as a result. One is thrilled with the business he gets by being involved. How can that be? Well, the two just belong and occasionally go to a meeting. The "winner" goes to every meeting, is active on a committee, sends a welcome letter to all new members, hosts a "mixer" once a year, etc.

On a local level, you can join the chamber of commerce, your neighborhood business group, a "lead club," Toastmasters, Kiwanis, Jaycees, or other business, civic, or special-interest groups. On a national level, you can participate in your industry's trade association.

Networking became a verb in the 1980s, and it is quite possibly the hottest proactive business-building technique of the 1990s. Because people naturally tend to do business with and refer others to people they know, trust, and like, nothing beats personally building relationships and rapport with influential people. The question, obviously, is how to cultivate relationships with people who might be helpful to you.

31

Basically, the power-networker becomes a resource to others. You know the best restaurants, the best travel agent, a contact at a local radio station or newspaper, a trustworthy broker, a friend in the mayor's office, etc. Gradually, you become a conduit of contacts and information; you help Joe meet Sam, Sam meet Joe, Sam and Joe meet Mary, and you can virtually count on receiving business, referrals, or other assistance from Joe, Sam, and Mary in return.

Cultivate these relationships through frequent personalized contact. When you meet someone you want to bring into your network, learn as much as you can about him or her, then make a point of mailing that person articles you notice that may interest him or her, occasionally a book, notice of an event, that sort of thing. Let's say you've met a successful insurance agent who knows a lot of businesspeople, and you believe networking with her could be good for your restaurant. Whenever you notice a particularly interesting article related to the insurance business, in the newspaper, in the *Wall Street Journal*, or in your restaurant industry magazines, tear it out, jot a note on the back of your business card ("Barb — thought this might interest you. John"), and drop it in the mail. If she comes to your restaurant, make a point of introducing her to another business owner/customer in a complimentary way: Harry, this is Barb Whizbang, one of the smartest insurance brokers in the Valley. Barb, this is Harry Nutsnbolts, the owner of the Gadget Manufacturing Company over on the North Side. This way, both of your customers appreciate the introduction. This is networking!

Let me give you an actual example. My chiropractor was talking with one of her patients about his business, making casual conversation, when that business owner mentioned his interest in finding somebody qualified to help him produce a television commercial for his product. My chiropractor told him about me and then called me and told me of the conversation. I got a good client, and the other patient, now my client, got a TV advertising campaign that has produced millions of dollars of revenue for his company. We are both grateful to the chiropractor for the introduction, and we have both gone out of our way to refer business and otherwise help that doctor. It's worth noting that the doctor's sincere interest in her patients' businesses, careers, families, and other activities is what makes these networking opportunities possible.

A good memory is very useful in networking. Being able to remember names, faces, and facts about people from conversations is an increasingly important business skill. There are a number of good books and courses on memory improvement, and it is worth your while to look into them if you need to improve your memory skills.

Here's a networking goal list you might want to adopt:

(a) Meet at least one new person each week, to add to your "million-dollar Rolodex." In a year, you'll add 52 people to your network.

(b) In person, by phone, or by mail, introduce one person to another, for their mutual benefit, every day. (If you were to eventually introduce each of the 52 people in your network to each of the others, you'd make over 2,500 introductions.)

(c) Mail a note, an article, or some other type of communication to at least 10 people in your network every week.

This kind of activity will yield tremendous benefits for you and your business.

b. GET OUT AND ABOUT

I know a chiropractor who, the month before opening his office, went out every day to nearby businesses, knocked on doors, introduced himself, and handed out his literature. It was a lot of hard, occasionally unpleasant work. He talked to over 2,000 people during that month, and when he opened the doors of his practice he immediately had dozens of new patients. They referred others, and he built a hugely successful practice without a dollar of advertising expense.

I think every small business owner ought to set aside a few days a month to visit neighboring businesses, area residences, if appropriate, and known prospects, if any, meeting and greeting them and passing out literature or coupons. You will spark some business and learn some things that will help you in your other marketing efforts.

c. EXHIBIT

Trade shows, fairs, neighborhood bazaars, shopping mall exhibits, and other exhibiting opportunities are outstanding ways to gain exposure inexpensively.

My chiropractor has obtained many new clients by giving free health check-ups at a health-food store, at a mall, at a health spa, and even at a swap meet! A kitchen remodeling company keeps itself busy all year round just from the leads and customers accumulated in two weeks of exhibiting at the annual state fair. A computer store gained over 100 new customers from exhibiting at one weekend business show.

For more on exhibiting, see *The Successful Exhibitor's Handbook*, another title in the Self-Counsel Series.

d. DO A SUPERIOR JOB AT INSIDE SALES

If customers come to your place of business, you need to be concerned with all aspects of inside sales — your business's appearance and environment, your merchandise display, your staff, the way your telephone is answered.

Here are some suggestions for evaluating your store design:

(a) Does the store present a congruent image? The look and "feel" of the store should be in keeping with the type of goods being sold, the price levels, the clientele, etc. A discount shoe store can have a different image from an upscale, specialty women's shoe store, for example. Each store's look and feel should reflect the image the owner has decided upon.

(b) Are the goods presented in a logical, organized way? Related merchandise needs to be grouped together.

(c) Do you use creative displays? I recently saw a display of camcorders in an electronics store, with a sign headlined "20 Ways You'll Use and Enjoy Your New Camcorder." This is smart suggestive selling, done silently, through creative displays and signs.

(d) Do you use displays that educate the customer about the products? You can use displays, live demonstrators, continuous-loop videos, or other means to educate your customers.

(e) Use every possibility and opportunity to promote, advertise, suggest, credibilize, and educate!

With regard to your staff, don't make the mistake many business owners make of hiring "clerks" and setting up expectations for them in keeping with the clerk position. You do not want clerks, you want salespeople, and you should interview, hire, train, manage, and compensate accordingly. If your business will not support sales-level base pay, then create bonus opportunities appropriate for superior performance. And, yes, you can hire inexperienced help and mold them into quality salespeople.

Your inside salespeople should be thoroughly familiar with your products and services and marketing messages, indoctrinated in customer service excellence, continually exposed to sales training through books, tapes, and meetings, and rewarded for top performance.

5

PUBLICITY

Publicity stunts used to be the norm in promoting products, businesses, and even Hollywood celebrities. There were publicity agents who got paid for dreaming up and implementing these stunts. Many of the entries in *The Guinness Book of World Records* are thanks to such publicity stunts. While stunts are not used as much today, publicity — essentially free advertising — is still hugely valuable, relatively easy to get, and well worth working on. This chapter will discuss some of the best paths to publicity.

a. CONNECT WITH A CAUSE

Many businesses link themselves to local or national causes, invent or sponsor fund-raising events, and donate from certain sales promotions, gaining considerable favorable publicity as a result.

As I write this, U.S. troops are coming home from the 1991 action in the Middle East and companies large and small are scrambling to gain favorable publicity by offering discounts, gifts, and services to the troops. This is happening to such a degree that the U.S. government has established a special ombudsoffice to coordinate it all.

AmericaWest Airlines gained a lot of local, positive publicity by giving free tickets to returning military personnel. In a five-day period, they were written up in the newspaper and mentioned repeatedly on all TV and radio news broadcasts. Other airlines have jumped on this bandwagon, too. A client of mine in the franchise business is shrewdly organizing his companies and other franchisors to offer special discounts and financing assistance to these returning troops. As a result, he's guaranteed a lot of great publicity.

If you can find a charity or cause that relates directly to your type of business, all the better. For example, a pet-supply store might donate doggy refreshments to a dog-walkathon that raises funding for guide dogs for the blind or a motorcycle dealership might permit use of its large lot to stage a motorcycle safety clinic. I do a little marketing consulting for the local Arthritis Foundation and its telethon and have played a role in securing a drugstore chain as a sponsor. For that chain, it's a perfect match: many older people will be interested in this particular telethon, and pharmacies want senior citizens as customers.

b. BE A PERSONALITY OR EXPERT

I often talk and write about Bob Stupak, the owner of the Vegas World hotel and casino in Las Vegas, as the classic model of a business owner creating publicity through his or her own persona. Stupak is often featured in newspapers and magazines, has been profiled on "60 Minutes," and, in total, has reaped millions of dollars worth of free advertising by being a notable, newsworthy, flamboyant personality. He has played high-stakes poker against a supposedly unbeatable poker computer, made the largest known bet on a boxing match at a competing casino — and won, and run for mayor of Las Vegas. Stupak has put his business on the map with the strength of his own personality.

You don't need to be eligible for "Lifestyles of the Rich and Famous" to take advantage of this type of publicity. In our area, there's a dentist who dresses up in a super hero costume once a week and speaks at schools' health classes as Super Dentist. Every so often, some TV newscast picks up on this and gives him some publicity.

If being a "personality" isn't your style but you qualify as an expert on some subject, you can use that to your advantage. Local and national media need a lot of quotable experts. If you can conduct a survey or poll, compile interesting statistics, make provocative predictions, or provide information on some timely news, you can get on radio and TV talk shows and be featured in newspapers and magazines. Every year at income tax time a number of accountants and other tax experts get tremendous amounts of free advertising, as they are sought out, interviewed, and quoted by the media. Instead of waiting for this to happen, you can find a way to make it happen.

One idea I gave to a florist was to compile statistics and lists of interesting and funny reasons why men come in and buy flowers, then let the media know that he had compiled all this information. In short order, he got interviewed on a local radio station and quoted in a local magazine. He sent that magazine article around to some national magazines, and wound up being quoted in one of the tabloids and in a national women's magazine. He has parleyed this into annual publicity at Valentine's Day time.

To become known as an expert, you can begin by writing some articles and having them published in your trade magazine or newsletter. With a few of these under your belt, you can approach your local newspaper with an idea for a story or a column (if you're really ambitious and confident). Your local paper may welcome free copy from someone who knows what he or she is talking about and can write. Volunteer to be a speaker for community groups. Every time you stand up in front of a group, people see you and accept you as an expert in the field you are lecturing on. With luck, your efforts will snowball: the more people see you as an expert, the more they want to use you as an authority for events, articles, and TV reports, and the more you are used as an authority, the better known as an expert you become.

c. PUBLICITY STUNTS

Yes, they still exist. On Friday the 13th, one of our local record stores erected a "superstition obstacle course" in its parking lot, complete with a ladder to walk under, a sidewalk crack to step on, mirrors to break, etc., and then dared all the radio and TV personalities to come down and go through the obstacle course. One radio station "bit" and did a live morning drive-time broadcast from the store's site, providing free advertising worth thousands of dollars.

A new country-western nightclub ran a "Dolly Parton look-alike contest" on Parton's birthday, and two out of the four local TV stations covered the event. Another nightclub did an "Elvis back from the dead" promotion on Halloween and got TV coverage, too.

d. HOLIDAY TIE-INS

There are many opportunities for you to link your business to holidays. People are very conscious of holidays, and the media look for ways to connect their reporting, talk show topics, and features to the holidays. The florist tying in his promotion to Valentine's Day is one example of this. Another would be a fabric store stocking novelty fabrics and costume patterns for Halloween and holding free sewing clinics on quick-sewing techniques throughout October.

For more discussion of promotion and publicity, see *Getting Publicity*, another title in the Self-Counsel Series.

6

LEARNING TO SELL

a. THE FOUR MYTHS ABOUT SELLING

Many business owners are reluctant to get going and sell. A lot of this reluctance seems to be rooted in a bad experience with a high-pressure, fast-talking salesperson or in the erroneous ideas that salespeople are disliked, not respected, and low on the prestige totem pole and that selling is difficult, unpleasant work.

1. Myth #1: To sell you have to pressure and manipulate people

That is one way to approach selling, and there are still a few types of products and businesses where this kind of tough selling is essential but, for the most part, the techniques often associated with the used car lot or door-to-door vacuum cleaner sales representative just do not wash in other applications and with today's consumer or businessperson. Instead, today, most selling is a polite process of finding people with problems, needs, or desires that you can offer good answers to.

2. Myth #2: People don't like or respect salespeople

I've been a salesman all my life and I have hundreds of friends as a result. In fact, it would be difficult to pick a sizable city in the United States or Canada where I couldn't phone somebody who would be delighted to pick me up at the airport and have lunch or dinner with me and, if I needed assistance, introduce me to his or her friends and contacts. Most people who have good sales skills and use them to help others get what they need or want in life have the respect and friendship of many people.

Being an assertive, dynamic sales representative for your own business is very likely to yield a lot of positive relationships as a by-product.

3. Myth #3: Being a salesperson lacks prestige

There's a very famous life insurance agent who specializes in serving (note the word *serving*) corporate executives. He flies to his appointments in one of his two private planes. His clients have their limousines pick him up at the airports. He is a trusted, much-relied-on, important financial adviser to his clients and their companies, on a par with their lawyers, accountants, and key associates. You would certainly have to conclude that, for him, selling is a very prestigious activity.

As an effective problem solver and a reliable adviser you can have all the prestige you might desire!

4. Myth #4: Selling is difficult, unpleasant work

It can be, but it definitely doesn't have to be! If you find ways to take creative, attractive messages and offers to people with a reason to be interested in what you have to say, your selling time can be very pleasant and rewarding.

b. THE VALUE OF SALES SKILLS

It's also important to remember that the development of an aptitude for selling is the mastery of human relations and communication. It will serve you well in every aspect of your life.

A powerful king called for a psychic. After a few minutes with his crystal ball, the psychic sadly delivered the bad news: "Sire, you will live to see your family and closest friends dead and buried." The king had this bearer of bad news taken to the dungeon, and called for another psychic — a second opinion. The second psychic, a salesperson at heart, reported: "Sire, you will be blessed with an extraordinarily long life."

Author Paul Parker would call that tact and skill in dealing with people. It is often called having "people skills." Whatever you want to call it, being able to persuade and motivate is a useful, desirable, and learnable skill.

Mark McCormack, author of the book *What They Don't Teach You at Harvard Business School*, said, "I believe most people are 'born salesmen.'"

Zig Ziglar, maybe American's best-known sales trainer, says "I've seen little baby boys and little baby girls, but I've never seen a little baby salesman — there are no born salesmen!"

They are both right. Ziglar makes the point that just about anybody can learn and master the skills of selling. I agree with that. I have seen the unlikeliest people grow into great salespeople when their need, their enthusiasm for what they are involved with, and their determination to succeed come together. There is abundant evidence against the idea that the ability or inability to sell is somehow genetic.

McCormack's point backs this up. He says that most people are "born salesmen" but then somehow learn how not to sell as they grow up. Most kids do have good sales instincts. They're certainly not afraid to ask for what they want, persistently and persuasively! You can re-kindle these instincts. Selling for your business can be fun!

c. MAKING A SALES CALL

Many business owners have opportunities to make personal sales calls, usually on other businesses. Here are some tips that will help you.

1. Preparation

First, it's useful to know something about the prospects you are going to call on. You may be targeting a particular type of business, for example, and be able to go to the library and read a few back issues of the trade magazines for that type of business, so you become familiar with its terminology, challenges, and issues. As a general rule of thumb, the more you know about your prospect or type of prospect, the better.

Second, you should prepare by practicing your presentation. Yul Brenner, who, I believe, gave more performances of *The King And I* than any other actor has ever given of a play, still rehearsed and practiced his part every day — he was a dedicated, consummate pro!

Third, you'll benefit from doing what athletes know as "getting up for the game." Mental attitude is important in selling. In fact, W. Clement Stone, an insurance magnate who built his sales empire in the depth of the great Depression, flatly stated: "The sale is contingent upon the attitude of the salesman."

Many sales pros like to listen to self-improvement or motivational audio-cassette tapes in their cars as they drive to their sales appointments. You might try this technique for a month and see what happens. After all, listening to the news or music on the car radio isn't contributing to your business success.

2. Professional image

Napoleon Hill, author of *Think and Grow Rich*, met Edwin C. Barnes shortly after Barnes formed his association with Thomas Edison — an association that would let Barnes retire to Florida, at quite a young age, as a multi-millionaire. Hill met Barnes not long after Barnes had made his way to Edison's factory by freight train because he could not afford the passenger fare. Yet Barnes had a large and expensive wardrobe, including 31 different suits, one for each day of the month. "I do not wear 31 suits entirely for the impression they make on other people," Barnes told Hill. "I do it mostly for the impression they have on me."

Hill later wrote in his book Laws of Success, "I have seen a few well-dressed people who made no outstanding records as salesmen, but I have yet to see the first poorly dressed man who became a star producer in the field of selling. I am firmly convinced that there is a close connection between clothes and success."

I have seen a few exceptions, but I generally agree: putting forth a positive, professional, successful image makes selling easier and more enjoyable. Right or wrong, most people — including your prospective customers — do judge books by their covers, cars by their hubcaps and hood ornaments, and people by their outward appearance.

Give careful consideration to the right image when selling for your business.

3.   Pleasant, friendly, courteous demeanor

No big secret here! By being pleasant and polite, you'll gain the co-operation of receptionists, secretaries, store clerks, and others, in obtaining information and getting in to see the business owners. I would sure appreciate your help, or I hope you can do me a favor, are phrases that have near-magical powers.

4.   Have a headline

Just as an advertisement needs a brief, concise headline that telegraphs the main benefit to be gained by reading the ad and using the advertised product, you need a similarly structured single sentence that describes what you want to talk with the business owner about. That sentence must focus on benefits to your prospect, not on what you want!

Let's say you are calling on businesses for your florist shop. Your headline might go something like this: "Our never-forget-an-important-occasion service and business discount plans may be of interest to you/the owner."

5.   Prepare a good, brief sales presentation.

There are many formulas or structures for a sales presentation, but the one I like best, seems to be the easiest to learn, and fits most businesses is "Problem/Agitate/Solve." To use this formula, you start by getting the prospect's agreement to certain problems. You fan the fire of those problems. Then you present your solution, emphasizing, of course, the best benefits you offer.

Using the florist shop again as the example, its owner, calling on a business owner, might say something like this:

> Ms. Owner, we know that you have personal gift-giving needs and important occasions to remember that are often a problem, as busy as you must be running the XYZ business. And forgetting an important birthday or anniversary or rushing to deal with such an occasion at the last minute isn't much fun, is it?
>
> That's why we invented our never-forget-an-important-occasion service, and provide it free of charge to business owners like you, along with special discounts. May I tell you a little more about this?

At that point, the florist has established and emotionalized a problem, offered a solution, and secured permission from the prospect to go ahead and present his services.

6. Make your offer and close

You will get some good results, over time, just by calling on prospects, making presentations like these, leaving literature, and moving on — but you'll get even better results if you have a definite, special offer to make and a deal to close.

Let's consider our florist again. After going through a full presentation of his services, he might close with this kind of offer:

> ...now here's our never-forget service registration form, for you or your secretary to fill in, with the dates of every important occasion, names of people you need to remember on those dates, and so on, along with a place for

your name, address, and credit card information for super-convenient telephone shopping. I'll leave this with you to be filled out, and pick it up on Friday. When I do, I'll be leaving a coupon booklet with over $100 in discounts as our new-client welcome gift. Then we'll be calling to remind you of every occasion, with a suggestion for that situation. Would it be better for me to pick this form up Friday morning or would afternoon be better?

7.   Good literature to leave behind

Whether you make a presentation immediately , arrange an appointment, or have to call back, you'll want to have a good piece of literature — probably a brochure — to leave behind.

Like the salesperson on a limited budget who wisely opts for getting just two very good suits instead of six cheap ones, you would be well advised to get one very good brochure prepared for your business. For many businesses, this will be a capabilities brochure, persuasively describing and illustrating your business, products, and services, and the benefits you provide. Literature cannot make the sale or get the customer, but it can establish you and your business as stable, reliable, successful, progressive, service-oriented, and worthy of consideration.

8.   Build a relationship

Your real object is not to make a sale but to establish a relationship. Regardless of the outcome of the appointment, immediately sending a thank-you note is a good move. Keeping that newly met person on your business's mailing list for months, or even up to a year, will pay off.

7

DISTRIBUTION

One of the most interesting things to me, as a consultant, is how many business owners limit themselves to getting sales through very few channels. I believe that diversity is the creative opposite of laziness and the best form of "failure insurance" there is. This chapter deals with various channels you can use to get sales for your products and services.

a. DIRECT-TO-THE-CONSUMER MARKETING

This means exactly what it says: with no or comparatively few intervening levels of distribution, you offer and sell your products directly to the consumer. In years gone by, the most popular method of direct-to-consumer marketing was door-to-door selling. Companies like Fuller Brush, Avon, and World Book Encyclopedia literally built empires with door-to-door sales organizations penetrating virtually every city, town, and community in North America. In business-to-business marketing, door-to-door or "cold canvassing" is still quite common today; sales representatives in the copier, FAX, computer, and other office equipment businesses, insurance, financial services, printing, and many other industries make sales calls on businesses and business owners.

If you are interested in developing a national direct-sales force, you can find directories of professional manufacturers' representatives and sales agencies at your public library, and, in most types of businesses, there are trade magazines in which you can advertise for sales representatives and in which sales

47

agents advertise, looking for additional product lines. Through magazines like Opportunity or Income Opportunities, you can recruit independent sales agents to sell to businesses or consumers. If you want to hire salaried or commissioned salespeople for a local area, you can use the Sales Help Wanted section of your city's newspaper. Or if you want to recruit independent sales agents, you may find using the Business Opportunities section of the newspaper more appropriate.

Another, increasingly popular although controversial form of direct selling is multi-level or network marketing. One of the best known, most successful, long-established companies using this method is the giant Amway Corporation. Amway markets its own line of hundreds of household, automotive, cosmetic, and nutrition products as well as MCI long distance telephone services, travel services, and many other goods and services, through an international network of independent distributors who not only sell but also recruit and manage others who sell and also recruit and manage others, etc.

Amway was started in 1959 in a garage by two friends with one product. Today, it is a multi-billion-dollar-a-year entity. Along the way it has inspired many other entrepreneurs and companies to try this multi-level approach, a few notably more successful than thousands of others.

There is a fine line between a legal network marketing approach and an illegal pyramid selling scheme; anyone thinking about using multi-level or network marketing should seek legal advice. For more details about multi-level selling, see *Get Rich Through Multi-Level Selling*, another title in the Self-Counsel Series.

Another variation of direct-to-consumer marketing is commonly called party plan selling. The giant in this field is Tupperware. This method has been used for selling jewelry, cosmetics, home decor items, cookware, home security systems, cruises, and vacations.

A version of party plan selling used in business-to-business marketing is the free introductory seminar or executive preview.

Still another type of direct-to-consumer marketing is direct mail, including sales letters, circulars, and catalogs. Direct mail can be used locally, regionally, nationally, or internationally.

b. RETAIL

Owning and opening your own retail store is probably the most common way of starting a small business and marketing products and services, and much of the material in these guides has been chosen to be particularly helpful to retail business owners.

Most people starting their own retail businesses have hopes for future expansion, through owning and opening additional outlets or by franchising based on their proven model. Franchising has made many entrepreneurs rich, and it will continue to be a relatively rapid path to wealth for many people.

To many, the investment of starting a retail store is overwhelming, and a growing trend is the sub-leasing of mini-stores within stores. For example, a chain of discount department stores leases small amounts of space to costume jewelry vendors and to candy and nut vendors, enabling the new entrepreneur to get started in one of those businesses just for the cost of inventory and rent deposits. Some stores, like this chain, do this as a regular part of their business, actively seeking lessee-operators for certain departments, and can be approached by interested entrepreneurs.

To other stores, it will be a new idea you will have to sell. Let's say you want to be in the business of conducting cooking classes and selling cookbooks and specialty cooking utensils. Instead of starting a full-blown store and dealing with a long-term lease, deposits, leasehold improvements, telephones, utilities, etc., you might strike a deal to rent a small but adequate amount of space from, say, an appliance store. The store gets rent plus a percentage of your sales, and benefits from customer traffic drawn in by your advertising and marketing. You get up and running for a lot less money and risk, and benefit from the customer traffic drawn in by the appliance store's advertising and marketing.

In some malls, there are also kiosk rental opportunities, where you have very limited space, bargain rent, and mall traffic. Some malls also offer short-term, Christmas-season-only rental spaces, which you might use to go into an appropriate business temporarily, evaluate the public's response, and make money that can be re-invested in establishing your business later on a more permanent basis.

c. WHOLESALE TO OTHER STORES

Many product marketers never have their own stores but sell, instead, through others' stores. If you are a manufacturer or prime source of a product, you will probably do this on a national basis, dealing with the main offices and buyers for various retail chains.

On a local level, however, you can also sell to other stores. For example, one owner of a muffin bakery and store has become the wholesale supplier of muffins to eight grocery stores in her area and, last year, sold over 25,000 muffins through those stores.

One way small manufacturers or wholesalers often get started is by placing their products on consignment in various stores and other retail outlets, often on racks or in self-contained display units. This means that the retail store owner only pays for the merchandise that is sold, as it is sold.

Many years ago, when eight-track tapes were just starting to die out in favor of cassettes and compact disks but many older cars and trucks still had eight-track players, one clever entrepreneur got the rights to produce eight-tracks from the music companies who were dropping out of that business themselves. He had eight-tracks duplicated, and set up routes at truck stops and gas stations throughout five states where he or his sales agents would place little counter-top displays of tapes on consignment. Every two weeks, his agents would go to each location, re-stock the displays, and collect for what was sold. As I recall, the tapes were sold to the customer for $7.00, sold to the retailer for $3.00, and cost about $1.30 to have produced, including royalties. In about five years, the business, which started with ten consignment locations, sold over a million tapes.

I know of another company that uses the same approach today with earring displays in beauty shops.

Different products are appropriate for selling to or through different types of retailers, but it pays to be creative about this. I once worked as a sales representative for a book publishing company and, when hired, was directed to call on and sell to all the bookstores, department store book departments, and card and gift shops in my territory. However, I soon learned that I could sell my company's cookbooks through restaurants and gourmet cooking equipment stores, the coloring books and game-books through toy stores, and a flower decorating book through gardening stores. Looking back, I could have done a great deal more with this than I did.

You can also market services through retail stores. Let's say you have a carpet cleaning business, and you have a friend who owns a high-traffic business like a dry cleaning business, car wash, drugstore, or supermarket. You could arrange to have a little display area in your friend's store, on the busiest days, probably Friday or Saturday, where you could display your equipment and before/after photos of jobs, demonstrate your cleaning technology, and line up prospects and book jobs with new customers. In one or two days of doing this, you might obtain dozens of new customers.

d. MARKETING TO MAIL-ORDER AND CATALOG COMPANIES

If you manufacture, import, or have exclusive rights to a product suitable for marketing through established mail-order companies' catalogs, you may be on your way to a fortune.

These companies are always looking for new products that will sell well in their catalogs, which they mail to large numbers of known mail-order buyers. If you can connect with them, you get the full force of their advertising and marketing expertise and their financial investment.

At your library, you can find directories of mail-order and catalog companies, pick those appropriate for your product, and contact them with a sales letter, brochure, or picture of the product and other information.

e. MARKETING AT TRADE SHOWS

Many inventors, manufacturers, importers, and entrepreneurs have got their big breaks at trade shows. You can gain distribution for a product through sales agents, through various types of stores, or through mail-order companies by exhibiting at the correct trade shows. There is at least one major trade show for virtually every type of business. For example, there are gift shows, toy shows, office supply shows, computer supply shows, and lawn and garden product shows. At your library you can find directories of trade shows. General business magazines like *Entrepreneur*, *Opportunity*, and *Income Plus* publish listings of upcoming shows, too.

It is even possible to go to a trade show with nothing but a prototype of your product and secure tentative deals.

Another reason to attend trade shows is to find new products to sell in your store or to your customers or even to find completely new business opportunities.

f. MARKETING THROUGH PUBLIC SHOWS AND FAIRS

If you have a demonstratable product for consumers or need to accumulate prospects for later follow-up, you will probably find terrific value in exhibiting at fairs, home shows in malls, and even swap meets or flea markets.

Some businesses travel a circuit of these kinds of events, and sell only at these events. There is a company that sells a special kind of protectant auto polish, for example, that has teams of demonstrators — commissioned salespeople — who work fairs and exhibitions all across the country, selling the auto polish on the spot. Last year, they sold over 250,000 cans of car polish with no stores, no in-store distribution, and virtually no overhead!

If you have a local business, you can benefit from the fairs and expos that come to your area. If I owned a restaurant, for example, I'd have a booth at a fair in my city, cooking, giving away samples of my best food specialties, giving away discount coupons, and collecting names and addresses via a free prize draw, so I could mail to them later.

g. SELLING A PRODUCT OR SERVICE AS A PREMIUM

A premium is something a marketer either gives away free or offers at a substantial discount in order to sell another product or service.

Many tangible products, including cookware, jewelry, vacation-club memberships, and appliances, are sold as premiums. One manufacturer of travel alarm clocks does over a million dollars a year selling clocks to companies that give them away free when they sell sets of luggage.

In my city, a windshield repair company has recently been using "a year's supply of dinners" at a popular local restaurant chain as a premium, to attract new customers. It's an odd mix, but it's working. And the restaurant owner selling the dinner certificates to the windshield repair company at a big discount is getting lots of new customers and valuable advertising.

A car wash owner made this deal with an auto dealership. The car wash owner sold to the dealer for $12 a coupon book with coupons good for 24 free basic washes. The car dealer advertised it and gave it away with any car sold or any service department work during the month of the promotion...the car wash got a lot of new customers *and* the profit from the add-on sales of wax and polish, tire cleaning, etc.

There may be many opportunities for you to package your services or products as premiums, for other businesses' use. It is worth looking into.

8

CUSTOMER SERVICE IS A
SALES ISSUE

The most important, productive, valuable asset you will ever possess in business is your customer. Everything else is replaceable. Businesses that mistreat or under-value their customers always eventually fail. Some may look successful for a while. Some will hang on longer than others. But ultimately they all die. I have very often predicted the demise of a business, months or even years in advance, even when it looked like it was doing well, based purely on my observation that its owners did not value their customers.

Once you have spent money advertising to bring a customer to you, to establish yourself in a convenient location, to ensure that your office or store is a good place to do business, to hire staff to look after customers, and to stock your inventory with good products, don't lose that customer because of poor customer service practices. That customer is far more valuable to you than just anyone out in the street — he or she has already indicated interest in buying by answering your ad or entering your store — so taking an "Oh, well, there are always more fish in the ocean" approach is just plain dumb. All your efforts up to this point have been directed at getting the customer to come into your store or answer your ad. What you have to do now is back up your ads and promises with some service and you will have a customer instead of a prospective customer.

a. MEETING AND EXCEEDING EXPECTATIONS

When I come home from traveling on speaking engagements and consulting assignments, and my wife or somebody in the office asks me about my trip, I do not tell them about the things that went as expected. (Those words "as expected" are very important.) Instead, I'm first likely to tell some horror story about an airline, car rental company, or hotel that treated me badly, often to the degree that, in retrospect, there's humor in the story. In other words, human nature guarantees I'll gripe first. And what I'm actually griping about is a merchant or supplier whose performance was significantly below my expectations.

The other thing I'm likely to talk about is what I call a miracle story — some business or person who treated me so nicely that I still have a tough time believing it really happened. In these rare cases, the merchant or supplier performed in a way that significantly exceeded my expectations.

For customer service that will be memorable for all the right reasons, you have to understand your customers' expectations and out-perform them. Here are the factors that control a customer's expectations:

(a) The customer's needs

(b) The customer's desires

(c) The business's advertising

(d) The market or competition

(e) What the customer knows about quality

(f) The business's externals — location, signage, etc.

(g) The customer's past experience

(h) The business's reputation

Recently, both my wife and a business partner had to have their cars repaired. His is a $60,000, one-year-old BMW; hers is a four-year-old Ford Taurus with 50,000 miles on it.

They both need their cars and had to have them fixed and back on the road as fast as possible. Yet they had very different expectations about what should happen.

My partner expected to either have his car fixed the same day or be given an appropriate loaner car. My wife expected to have her car in the shop for several days and hoped for a discount on a rental car.

My partner wanted (and expected) VIP treatment. My wife wanted only a promise of when her car would be fixed and to have that promise kept.

What set up this gap in their expectations?

BMW currently uses the advertising slogan "the precision driving machine," and my partner's BMW has been anything but that. He believed the advertising and the sales representative's linked promises about the dramatically superior quality and reliability of this particular car. Now he is easily disappointed.

The competitive, comparable luxury automobiles he could have bought are also advertised as precision-crafted and remarkably reliable, and that further fixes in his mind the idea that his car should perform flawlessly.

In this case, the price difference between products is perceived by both consumers as a clear indication of a quality difference. He believes that paying a high price — $35,000 more than the price of his previous cars, my car, or my wife's car — entitles him to a better product and to much better service from the seller.

The image of the BMW dealership itself is up-scale, more like the image of a jewelry store than of a service station, and it, too, communicates that he should get some very special service here.

My partner's past experience with Lincoln-Continentals and Cadillacs, and with the dealerships that sold and serviced those cars, had been quite good. Other people bragging about their BMWs also influenced his feelings.

Ford's advertising for the Taurus was not much of a factor in my wife's original purchasing decision. And the current advertising for that car and for the local dealership really doesn't promise much of anything — it is built on vague generalities, not specific claims or comparisons against other cars.

My wife's idea of the inherent quality in her car is that it is supposed to be a good, reasonably reliable car. Knowing she has put 50,000 miles on the car, she expects things to go wrong and is not all that upset when they do.

She has dealt with three different Ford dealerships' service departments and several different service stations over the years and would tell you that one is pretty much the same as the other. The dealerships' service departments look like repair shops and nothing much more. Her past experiences with Ford cars and the dealerships has been good but not exceptional. Most conversations she has with her friends and coworkers about cars, car dealers, and car repair services is negative and critical, serving to lower her own expectations.

When you consider all this, it becomes clear that it is much easier for the Ford repair people to satisfy or favorably impress my wife than for the BMW people to satisfy or favorably impress my business partner. In actuality, the BMW people went on to so thoroughly anger my business partner that he's ready to get rid of the car after having it for only a year, even if he loses money on it, and will undoubtedly never buy a BMW product again. The Ford people satisfied my wife, she has good things to say about the dealership, and she will probably trade her car in there and buy another Ford.

This is not to suggest that BMW should strategically act to lower their customers' expectations. Instead, they should recognize that with the sale of very expensive automobiles advertised as "precision driving machines" comes a certain special level of responsibility.

Both manufacturers and certainly both dealers had the opportunity to understand their customers' differing expectations and then work to exceed them. My business partner has a great many bad things to say about this BMW dealership and is saying them to anybody who'll lend a sympathetic ear. The damage he's doing right now to this business is incalculable, all because their performance came in so dramatically below his expectations. My wife has modestly good things to say about the Ford dealer, and is only saying them when prompted by somebody. She isn't doing that business any damage but isn't doing it any real good either, because their performance only matched her expectations.

b. MAKING MONEY FROM REFERRALS

One great result of expectation-exceeding customer service is positive word-of-mouth advertising. It is better to gain a customer as a result of referral from another, established, satisfied customer than through commercial advertising, for reasons including the following:

(a) Lower marketing cost. Obviously, it costs less to get a referral than to get a customer through advertising. In many cases, it's free or virtually free.

(b) Less price resistance. Customers referred by satisfied customers come with a certain level of pre-established trust. They are predisposed to buy. And they'll be less resistant to price than new customers attracted by advertising.

(c) More referrals. The customer obtained as a referral is much more likely to, in turn, refer than is the advertising-generated customer. Many businesses have endless chains of referrals: Mary refers Bob who refers Susan...and so on.

For these reasons, it is worth your while to work at stimulating referrals. Jerry Wilson's book *Word-of-Mouth Advertising* provides a detailed, step-by-step plan of action for stimulating referrals. Wilson coined the term "The Talk Factor" to represent the impact of word-of-mouth advertising, and he says that talk (about a product, service, or business) is not an uncontrollable intangible but a measurable, collectible, manageable commodity that can move results to the bottom line just like any other marketing tool. In other words, word-of-mouth advertising can be managed.

Even though I once owned an ad agency and have continued as an advertising copywriter and consultant for many years, I believe that many businesses can be built entirely through managed word-of-mouth advertising.

If you want lots of word-of-mouth advertising, it's just not enough to be adequate. As I pointed out in my story about returning home from trips, I don't talk about service that only meets my expectations, only about the kind that fails to meet or significantly exceeds my expectations.

In the story about the two cars' repairs, both dealers missed opportunities to sell cars through word-of-mouth advertising, by doing business with those two people without delivering performance that dramatically exceeded those people's expectations.

Often, getting from adequate/good customer service, which creates few or no referrals, to exceptional customer service, which dramatically exceeds customer expectations and creates many referrals, involves "little things." Try using a "one little thing" program in your business. In one tire shop I know, each employee is required to find "one little thing" to fix, free of charge, on each car. When the customer picks up the car, this repair appears on the invoice as a no charge. The customer's expectations, focusing on proper repair work and reasonable charges, are significantly exceeded. The customer gets a pleasant surprise to help him or her get over

60

the always-nasty business of looking at the invoice and paying it.

I teach the chiropractors and dentists who attend my practice-building seminars to make "concern calls." At the end of each day, they take a few minutes to call at home new patients or patients who were in and had particularly severe pain or problems that day, just to ask if they're okay. Invariably, the doctors get referrals from many of these patients within a few weeks. Because their "concern call" exceeded the patients' expectations, referral action was stimulated — it's that simple!

Not long ago, I was staying in a Hilton Hotel, got in late and weary, and ordered a room service meal. About ten minutes after its delivery, I got a "concern call" from the restaurant manager, just checking to make sure my meal was okay. Maybe there's a way you can adapt this idea to your business.

These kinds of "little things" can make a big difference in just about any business. Here are some tips for getting maximum positive word-of-mouth advertising and referrals:

(a) Make it a marketing and management priority.

(b) Become a serious student of word-of-mouth advertising.

(c) Define your customers' expectations. Keep amending and adding to the list as your understanding of your customers grows.

(d) Set up a plan to consistently exceed those expectations.

(e) Look for new ways to exceed customer expectations.

(f) Implement the "little things program" idea.

(g) Ask your customers, through surveys, questionnaires, conversation, etc., about what they need, want, like, and don't like. One large supermarket invites customers in to Saturday meetings, to discuss their likes and dislikes and what could be done better in the store.

(h) Measure the success of your word-of-mouth advertising. Keep track of the number of referrals you get in total and the percentage of your customers who do refer.

c. HANDLING COMPLAINTS

Times will inevitably occur when your business fails to meet customer expectations. If you are lucky, this will result in complaints. Yes — if you are lucky you will get complaints. Most unhappy customers do not complain; they simply walk away and resolve never to spend their money at your business again. Then, you have lost not only a customer (and all the potential customers he or she will warn away) but the chance to learn from the situation and improve your business so that the problem does not occur again. If your customer does complain, you have the chance to "make it right" for the customer, send that customer away convinced that you are the best business in town, and resolve the problem in your business.

Customer complaints give you one of your best opportunities to go beyond the ordinary in customer service and win over the customer. Unfortunately, too many businesses do not see it that way. They think of complaints as a bother or an unjustified attack on their business. Don't make this mistake.

One unhappy customer can do damage that a dozen satisfied customers cannot mend. For some perverse reason, we all tend to gripe about our unhappy consumer experiences more than we tell others about our satisfactory experiences. The horror stories are more fun to tell. Telling them lets us vent our frustrations and irritation. So, if you alienate a customer, you can count on dozens of people hearing about it. Thus, the prevention of and effective management of complaints is a marketing function.

Some years ago, while CEO of a manufacturing firm, I got a phone call on a Friday morning from a deservedly irate customer; we had improperly labeled his audio cassettes, and he had a speaking engagement that weekend he needed that product for. He now had no choice but to distribute incorrectly labeled merchandise. He wasn't our biggest customer; in fact, he was one of our smallest. He was not, by purely monetary standards, a VIP.

After his call, I mobilized as best I could. I stopped all other production in the factory in order to duplicate his order and get it to the airport by late afternoon. I flew it in so that it arrived in the customer's city that night. I arranged for a messenger service at the other end to get it, store it overnight, and deliver it to the hotel where the customer's seminar was the next morning, so it was waiting for him when he got there. I also immediately called a steak company and arranged to have a great selection of steaks reach his office on Monday, via Federal Express, with a note of apology for causing him anxiety and inconvenience. The whole, massive correction actually cost us more than the entire value of the order. And, at the time, the company could ill afford the expense. I tell the story not to brag or self-aggrandize, but to illustrate how much importance I place on preserving customer satisfaction.

That customer, incidentally, subsequently became one of our company's top twenty customers and, more important, became a goodwill ambassador, praising us to anybody who'd listen. He was worth at least $100,000 to us in referral business, and he remains a periodic consulting client of mine today, some ten years later.

Of course, there are times when the customer is actually wrong, so outrageously wrong that your only choice is to sacrifice him or her and all those he or she may poison. Bill Cosby once said "I'm not sure what the secret of success is — but I do believe the secret of failure is trying to please everybody." But preventing the creation of a "bad-will ambassador" must be a top priority.

Another story. I was a goodwill ambassador for a particular car dealership for nearly ten years, buying all my family and business vehicles there, referring dozens of customers, and praising it by name from the public platform in speeches and seminars. In total, I delivered at least a quarter of a million dollars in direct business to that dealership and maybe four times that much indirectly.

Foolishly, this dealership's car rental department gave me a lot of aggravation over nothing. I won't bore you with the details. Take my word for it — they were way out of line. I wrote the dealership manager a detailed letter about the situation. He called and essentially said there was nothing he could do about it. Actually, there were at least five different things I can think of he could have done, but he chose to do nothing. Until he made that choice, I was so committed to that dealership that I would never even have thought about buying another brand of car or a car anywhere else; I actually would have felt disloyal and guilty if I had. But at that moment he released me from that commitment. Since then, two friends have bought new cars, and I never opened my mouth to suggest they visit this dealership.

Now here's something to think about. Let's say that it costs that car dealership about $250 to get a new customer. That's what they spend in advertising, promotion, marketing, etc., to get each new customer. They could have spent $249 to pacify me and been a buck ahead.

I know businesspeople who'll spend $1,000 a month on a Yellow Pages ad to get a few new customers but will fight to the death and lose an established customer over a nickel. Not smart.

d. YOUR COMPLAINT RESOLUTION AND PREVENTION PROGRAM

As a marketing function of your business, you need both a complaint prevention program and a complaint correction, fast-response program.

Complaint resolution steps vary widely from one business to another. For example, in the skin care and ics salons business I own an interest in, the policy con a customer complaint about the actual effects of the p is to bring it to top management immediately, because a person with a rare allergic reaction could need guidance. There are risks of lawsuits, and, even though we are insured, why invite such serious problems? When you are dealing with products people apply to their skin, a high level of caution and concern is necesary.

On the other hand, in my publishing business, my policy is that I do not even want to hear about complaints unless the staff is unable to resolve them. There are several layers of staff between the complaint and me, and usually I only see complaint statistics every few months. The two companies are about the same size, by the way, so it's not size dictating different policies but the nature of the businesses.

Here are some general points you should consider when drafting your policy for handling complaints:

(a) Don't argue with the customer. When you or your employee is listening, writing down facts, and accepting the complaint, and the customer is complaining, the temperature of the conflict is not getting worse and may get better. Often, the complainer will blow off a lot of steam, wind down, and become reasonable all of his or her own accord. But any argument only serves to fan the flames, send the temperature through the roof, and heighten the difficulty of getting to a resolution.

(b) The person facing the complainer or taking the complaint call should have as much authority as possible, so he or she can assure the customer that something will be done. In some businesses, there are set parameters that staff members can operate within to resolve complaints on their own.

(c) The faster the complaint can be resolved, the better. While Joe Customer waits, he can work himself up and convince himself that he is in for a real fight. By having a fast response and resolution plan for your business, you eliminate this part of the problem.

(d) The decision not to resolve a complaint should never be made without the owner's or top manager's knowledge.

(e) When you do resolve a complaint reasonably and amicably, if you want to keep that person as a customer, it's perfectly appropriate to again solicit his or her business, by mail, by phone, or in person. When I was running a manufacturing business, I sent a letter like the one in Sample #3 on more than one occasion.

For more about customer service, see *Keeping Customers Happy*, another title in the Self-Counsel Series.

Joe Customer
123 Complaint Lane
Upset, Missouri
54321

Dear Mr. Customer,

I'm glad we were able to correct the error made in producing your widgets last week, get a rush shipment to you, and resolve this problem satisfactorily. Your patience and cooperative commitment to a solution (not a conflict) was very much appreciated. Please accept the enclosed coupon for a free dinner at any MMM-MMM! Steak House as a thank-you gift.

Also, let me again give you my personal assurance that your experience was a real aberration — not the norm in working with us. As you can see from the enclosed client reference list, we provide service to many of the leaders in your type of business, and many of these clients order from us frequently. Our ability to satisfy them is based on an overall 3.8 percent defect rate (the lowest in this industry) and a 98 percent on-time delivery record.

I hope we'll have another opportunity to do business in the future. Enclosed is a $500 savings certificate good toward any future order of $3,000 or more. Please call Will Pleez in Account Services or me, personally, if we can be of service to you.

Sincerely,

Humble Owner

9

MANAGING TO MAXIMIZE SALES

a. YOUR CUSTOMER LIST

I almost bought a bookstore once, but I walked away from the deal as soon as I discovered that no mailing list existed of the store's customers.

Whatever kind of business you are in, you must build, maintain, and use a customer list. Famous bank robber Willie Sutton was once asked why he kept robbing banks, and he answered, "That's where the money is." Well, in business, the money is in the customer list. It is your most important and valuable asset.

At bare minimum, you should acquire names, addresses, and telephone numbers. If you market to consumers or individual executives, you may also want to compile their birthday and anniversary dates, kids' names and birthdays, pets' names, and other "friend information." If you market to businesses, you may want several different names and titles.

"Out of sight, out of mind" is a great warning for marketers. There is tremendous competition for the attention, interest, enthusiasm, and money of every customer. And how easily customers forget! You cannot take customer loyalty for granted.

I think you start in this area at the very beginning of the relationship with each new customer. When a relationship starts right, it's likely to continue moving along in a positive direction. Sample #4 is based on a letter I received from a mail-order firm a few days after placing an order. If you were me and received this letter, how would it make you feel? Even knowing it must be a form letter, wouldn't it still make you feel good about having placed an order with this company? Even a simple but formal thank-you has immense power, because it is, unfortunately, so rare.

Many businesses compile their customer lists from their invoices or sales receipts or simply ask customers to sign up on the mailing list to receive notices of sales, special events, and new products. If you want to go a step further, you can have a monthly prize draw for all new customers who sign up during the month, give coupons for future purchases to each person whose name goes onto your mailing list, or offer a free monthly or bi-monthly newsletter. It is usually very easy to add names to your mailing list, but most business owners just don't think about doing it.

For most businesses, I believe there should be at least ten to twelve contacts per year with each customer, in addition to actual transacted business. These contacts may be in the form of a customer newsletter, a birthday card, holiday greetings, phone calls, or whatever. The periodic contact is intended to keep your business on the mind of your customer.

Beyond that minimal level of list use, you can use mailings to your past and established customers to stimulate business. In direct marketing and in mail order, your own list, called a house list, will be many times more responsive than any outside lists. Still, most mail-order companies err in mailing offers to their own customers too infrequently. I believe the same principle is true for every type of business: there's a lot of neglected opportunity in your own customer list!

b. WHAT DOES TIME MANAGEMENT HAVE TO DO WITH MARKETING?

When I took over the reins of a particularly troubled, struggling, money-losing company, its outgoing president said to me, "Your toughest challenge will be getting out from under

SAMPLE #4
ORDER THANK-YOU LETTER

Elf's Christmas Goodies Ltd.
123 Little People Road
Leprechaun, Indiana
54321

December 2, 199-

Mr. Dan S. Kennedy
987 Entrepreneur Boulevard
Success, Kansas
12345

Re: Order No. 70139

Dear Mr. Kennedy:

It was a pleasure to receive your fine order. Thank you for giving us the opportunity to serve you.

All instructions have been carefully noted; shipment will be made accordingly.

Your order is sincerely appreciated. I personally assure you it is receiving our very best attention.

Best wishes for an enjoyable holiday season.

Sincerely,

J.W. Elf
Elf's Christmas Goodies Ltd.

the b.s. once in a while, long enough to get something sold." And I have to tell you — he was right! It is alarmingly easy to get so absorbed in all the non-marketing details and problems of a business that you never find the time to get anything sold.

A real estate agent named Ron Rush consistently sells more residential real estate than any other real estate sales-person in America. It's interesting that he talks more about time management than about sales and marketing tech-niques. He has learned that he has to have procedures, sys-tems, disciplines, rules, and self-management methods that give him the time he needs to sell. I think the business owner has to invest at least 25 percent of his or her time in sales and marketing.

Another way to look at this is to determine what each of your hours has to be worth in order to achieve your earnings goals. Table #1, based on eight-hour workdays, shows you —

(a) What each hour has to be worth, to achieve certain annual earnings.

(b) What each minute has to be worth, to achieve certain annual earnings.

(c) What one hour a day is worth in a year.

Everybody says "Time is money," but how many people act on that truth? In Las Vegas, they cleverly take away your real money and give you brightly-colored chips to play with. This is not caprice on the casino operators' part. People tend to risk more, lose more, and lose more cheerfully when operating with play money than with the form of money they deal with in everyday life.

Similarly, because minutes, quarter hours, half hours, hours, and days are not dispensed in the form of coins and bills, it's hard for us to feel the same way about spending time as we do about spending money. The same person who gets confused in a dark cocktail lounge and leaves a $50 tip when he or she meant to leave $5, and feels awful about doing so, will think

TABLE #1
IS TIME MONEY?

IF YOU WILL EARN	EVERY HOUR IS WORTH	EVERY MINUTE IS WORTH	AN HOUR A DAY FRITTERED AWAY WILL COST YOU IN A YEAR
$ 20,000.00	$10.25	$0.1708	$ 2,500.00
$ 30,000.00	$15.37	$0.2561	$ 3,750.00
$ 50,000.00	$25.61	$0.4269	$ 6,260.00
$100,000.00	$51.23	$0.8523	$12,500.00

nothing about wasting an hour waiting in line or chatting around the water cooler. Yet one loss is as bad as the other.

In my own speaking, consulting, and TV production businesses, I am both the marketer and the service provider, and am always wrestling with the allocation of time to fulfill existing contracts and satisfy today's clients versus to make sure that there are new clients and new projects coming on board next week and next month and next year. In my kinds of businesses, you can be so busy this week you can't breathe but be looking at a frighteningly blank calendar just a few weeks down the road. I have to make time for marketing, or I'll be wildly successful this month but out of business next month.

My business is not unique in this. Every businessperson who somehow participates in the delivery of services must balance time between that job function and prospecting and marketing. Every restaurant owner must allocate time to supervising menus, meal preparation, personnel, and customer service as well as to marketing functions. You cannot let circumstances or other people control this division of your time and attention. You must do it by deliberate plan.

As you wrestle with time management, you'll undoubtedly want to do some extra reading and maybe even attend a seminar or two on the subject, and I'd encourage that. But I have made quite an in-depth study of time-management strategies, and find that most experts' recommendations and systems focus on 10 strategies:

(a) Use daily to-do lists

(b) Control clutter

(c) Use tickler files

(d) Streamline your correspondence

(e) Delegate

(f) Block time

(g) Operate off peak

(h) Get and use good tools

(i) Eradicate time wasters

(j) Manage the information explosion

1. Use daily to-do lists

If you get into the habit of making and using lists, you'll take a giant leap forward in getting better value from your time. Personally, I like to make my "to do" and "people to call" lists the night before. Many people number the items on their lists by priority (1 — most important, 2 — second most important, etc.) and a lot of experts advise sticking to the completion of number 1 before moving on to number 2. If you can make this work for you in the entrepreneurial environment, I'll stand up and applaud you. I do such numbering and use it as a guide, but I find that rigidly sticking to completing one item before moving on to the next is often just not practical. For that reason, I also use a second way of ranking items: A, B, and C. A items are those that must get done today or life on this planet ends; B items are those that it would be very good to get done, but that are not of life or death importance; and C items are options — if they are done today, that's fine, but if they are carried over until tomorrow, that's okay too. Most days I get through the As and a few Bs. Every once in a while I have what I call a "clear the decks" day and get through all the As, Bs, and accumulated Cs.

I find there's a benefit to all this beyond organization and efficiency: marking completed items off the list has a motivating and energizing effect.

2. Control clutter

The most creative and the most successful people I know work at keeping clutter to a minimum. Clutter consumes time through confusion and saps energy. Good filing systems, storage containers, shelves, project notebooks — all these things make a positive contribution to your productivity.

3. Use tickler files

Tickler files are set up according to calendar days and months. My own system is fairly common: I have 93 file folders labelled red 1 to 31, blue 1 to 31, and yellow 1 to 31. Red is the current month, blue is the next month, and yellow is the month after that. These tickler files — called that because they "tickle" the memory — clear my desk of clutter, free my mind of things and dates to remember, and organize my life every day. At the end of each day, I take the next day's folder, and everything I need is right there, waiting.

I use these files in the following way.

Crossing my desk today will be —

(a) A bill from my publisher for a shipment of books I got last week.

(b) A bill from my travel agency.

(c) A catalog with something in it I'd like to order for my wife, for Christmas.

(d) Coupons for restaurants in Las Vegas.

(e) A letter from a prospective client about a meeting in September that we need to schedule.

(f) A proposal for a TV infomercial to look at.

I'm rushing around this morning, getting ready to go to the airport for a three-day trip. Here's what I do:

(a) The publisher's bill is due in 30 days. Today is August 1. I drop it into the red 30 file folder and forget it.

(b) The travel bill is due in ten days. I drop it into red 9 and forget it.

(c) The catalog goes in yellow 30, to pop up October 30.

(d) I'm going to Las Vegas late in September, but I'm not sure when yet, so the Vegas coupons go in blue 15, to pop up September 15, probably a few days in advance of that trip.

(e) The client letter goes in blue 1, to pop up on September 1. (I also make a note, "blue 1," on that client's card in my card file, so that if some action occurs on this matter before then I can easily find the letter.) Then I forget it.

(f) The proposal goes in red 5, the first day I'll be back in the office with time to review it and, until then, I forget it.

4. Streamline your correspondence

If you respond to a lot of correspondence, inquiries from prospective customers, etc., you must develop form letters. If you use a computer, all the standard or form letters and paragraphs for letters can be stored in the computer and chosen by number, and letters can be produced very quickly. If you do not have a computer, you can develop a collection of fully prepared form letters you can just add the individual's name to and then send out.

Many business leaders have the habit of just handwriting short responses to letters right on the letters and returning them, without the formality of a typed reply. Personally, I favor this method when dealing with people with whom you have an established relationship. It works very well when you transmit the reply by fax; the whole letter then stays as your file copy.

5. Delegate or stagnate

I heard Jay Van Andel, the co-founder of the Amway Corporation, give a speech with that title over 15 years ago and I've never forgotten the thought.

Delegating is very difficult for the entrepreneur. By nature, we're Lone Rangers. We want things done our way. But a real sign of personal growth and maturity is the recognition that there often is more than one right way. And you will quickly find yourself running out of time every day if you do not learn to delegate. You literally have to "delegate or stagnate."

6. Block time

Many people fall into the trap of going into the office or store every day and just reacting to each call, visitor, or event. That's employee behavior, not entrepreneur behavior.

I block time by scheduling inviolate appointments with myself for certain important activities. For example, the way I get my books written is to schedule days where I do nothing but stay home and write; no other appointments or calls can be scheduled for that day once it is blocked for that purpose.

I encourage chiropractors to block a half day a week to close the office and do outside marketing activities like personally calling on their business neighbors, doing public speaking, and giving free health check-ups at a nearby health food store or spa. If doctors try to fit in these activities when there's time, there just never seems to be any time to fit them into!

7. Operate off peak

If I drive from my house to my office between 7:30 and 9:00 a.m., it takes about 40 minutes to get there. If I drive there after 9:00 (or before 7:30), it's a 10-minute trip. By setting up my schedule so I make that trip "off peak," I gain 30 minutes a day.

This idea can be applied to other situations: avoid the bank on Friday afternoons; avoid the post office the day after the rate increases and issuance of new stamps; avoid restaurants during dinner rush. All this adds up.

8. Get and use good tools

Depending on your business activities, a portable cellular phone, fax machine, dictating machine, and personal computer may pay for themselves in time savings. For me, having a fax machine at home as well as at the office has saved an enormous amount of time and allowed me to be much more productive this year.

9. Eradicate time wasters

Different people are plagued by different types of time wasters. I rarely agree to meet anyone at a restaurant for a lunch meeting any more; I learned that I'd be on time but that they'd keep me waiting for 15 to 20 minutes. Now I insist that they come to my office and we go from there. While they keep me waiting, I can get a phone call or other task completed and off my list!

For many business managers, meetings are big time wasters. I've developed a little regimen for keeping meetings' consumption of time under control:

(a) Say no. Don't go if you don't have to.

(b) Delegate — send somebody else.

(c) Use other, briefer communication options. Conference calls let you hold or attend meetings without leaving your place of business.

(d) Plan and prepare, and insist others do the same. I try never to go to a meeting without an agenda.

(e) Have stand-up meetings in your office.

(f) Make the meeting come to you, so you can work until it starts and get back to work as soon as it ends.

Whatever the reoccurring time wasters are in your days, there are solutions to be found or invented.

10. Manage the information explosion

Abraham Lincoln is quoted as saying "If I had five hours to chop down a forest, I'd spend the first three sharpening my axe." We can never get so busy that we can't "sharpen the axe."

There is a wealth of information out there, and the more of it you can process, the better. Here are my tips for handling the information explosion:

(a) Improve your reading skills. Speed reading allows you to maintain an excellent level of comprehension while you are reading fast. I read at least two new books every week, and couldn't do it if I weren't an accomplished speed reader. You can probably find a speed-reading course at a local community college or private learning center.

(b) Read what's important; skip what isn't. I don't really read the *Wall Street Journal*, for example; I go through it to find items of importance to me, tear them out, and throw away the rest of the paper immediately.

(c) Use driving time to listen to audio cassettes. Book and magazine summaries, novels, non-fiction books, newsletters, seminars, and how-to courses on every imaginable topic are now available on cassette. Just driving to and from your place of business and running a few errands, you'll put in about 350 hours a year behind the steering wheel. Audio cassettes turn that commuting time into learning time.

All of this is doubly important if you are moving from a very structured, controlled work environment to being your own boss. If you're used to being told what to do and when to do it, suddenly being adrift without that kind of supervision and direction can be a real shock to your system! Using these 10 time management keys can be of great help in managing yourself.

For more helpful hints about how to manage your time, see *Practical Time Management*, another title in the Self-Counsel Series.

c. HOW TO HIRE OUTSIDE EXPERTS

Ad agencies. Public relations firms. Telemarketers. Consultants. You are going to have plenty of opportunities to sign checks for their services. Be very cautious and conservative in choosing and investing in these experts. The temptation is to get responsibility off your shoulders by jumping at the first of these people to come along and promise you the moon. But successful business owners resist this temptation.

When you do have good reason to use these kinds of outside experts, here are some tips to keep in mind:

(a) Check references.

(b) Shop around. Look for people with experience or background directly relevant to your type of business. Given two ad agencies with basically the same qualifications, one with people who have succeeded in helping a business similar to yours and the other with nobody on staff with such experience, why choose the one where your wheel would have to be reinvented from scratch?

(c) Be very clear about your objectives.

(d) Be an open-minded listener, and carefully consider all suggested ideas, but, ultimately, trust your own understanding and instincts about your business.

APPENDIX
RECOMMENDED READING

a. BOOKS

Kennedy, Dan S., *The Ultimate Sales Letter*. Holbrook, MA.: Bob Adams Inc., 1990.

Kotler, Philip, *Principles of Marketing*. New Jersey: Prentice-Hall, Inc., 1980.

Levinson, Jay Conrad, *Guerrilla Marketing*. New York: Houghton Mifflin Company, 1985.

Ogilvy, David, *Ogilvy on Advertising*. New York: Crown Brooks, 1983.

Trout, Jack, and Al Reis, *Marketing Warfare*. New York: McGraw-Hill, 1986.

____ *Positioning: The Battle for Your Mind*. New York: McGraw-Hill, 1986.

Wilson, Jerry. *Word-of-Mouth Advertising*. New York: Wiley & Sons, 1991.

b. MAGAZINES

Advertising Age, Crain Communications, Inc., Chicago, IL.

AdWeek, A/S/M Communications, Inc., New York, NY.

American Demographics, American Demographics, Inc., Ithaca, NY.

Business Marketing, Crain Communications, Inc., Chicago, IL.

c. MEDIA DIRECTORIES

Bacon's Publicity Checkers, Bacon's Publishing Company, Chicago, IL.

Broadcasting/Cablecasting Yearbook, Broadcasting Publications Inc., A Times-Mirror Company, Washington, D.C.

Canadian Advertising Rates and Data, Mclean Hunter, Ltd., Toronto, Ontario.

Standard Rate and Data Service, Standard Rate and Data Service, A MacMillan, Inc. Company, Chicago, IL.

d. EXPERT HELP

- I conduct half-day seminars throughout the United States, called The Small Business Emergency Survival Workshops, which provide an in-depth look at how small businesses can use direct mail effectively. We go through five different models: a restaurant, a retail shop, a service business, a professional practice, and a manufacturer marketing to other businesses. The seminar, along with sample direct-mail campaigns, fill-in-the-blank sales letters, and computer software, has been packaged up in kit form. If you'd like information about these kits or about when the seminar is coming to your area, write or call my office.

  I am also available for speaking engagements and consulting assignments. As well, information about my audio cassettes, courses, and newsletters is available from my office:

    Kennedy & Associates
    5818 North 7th Street, #103
    Phoenix, Arizona   85014

- The best expert on Yellow Pages advertising that I know is Chris Newton, who publishes an entire home study course for Yellow Pages advertisers, called "Turning Yellow Into Gold." If you'd like information about it, write to me at my office.

- The Memory Company in Atlanta, Georgia, puts on memory skills seminars throughout the U.S. and

Canada, and offers a home study course, too. You may want to write to this company for information.

8351 Roswell Road, #329
Atlanta, Georgia 30350
(404) 552-0882

- Dr. Konopacki is a nationally recognized expert in successfully profiting from exhibiting. I would urge you to get his information and tips before exhibiting for your business.

    Dr. Allen Konopacki
    Incomm Center for Sales Training
    1005 North La Salle Drive
    Chicago, Illinois   60610

- Jerry Wilson, author of *Word-of-Mouth Advertising*, also conducts seminars about "The Talk Factor." Telephone him at 1-800-428-5666 or (317) 257-6876 for more information or to order his book.